AMERICAN CORN

TRUE STORIES

AMERICAN CORN

TED MALINOWSKI

TATE PUBLISHING
AND ENTERPRISES, LLC

Published by Tate Publishing & Enterprises, LLC
127 E. Trade Center Terrace | Mustang, Oklahoma 73064 USA
1.888.361.9473 | www.tatepublishing.com

Tate Publishing is committed to excellence in the publishing industry. The company reflects the philosophy established by the founders, based on Psalm 68:11,
"The Lord gave the word and great was the company of those who published it."

Book design copyright © 2013 by Tate Publishing, LLC. All rights reserved.
Cover design by Joel Uber
Interior design by Deborah Toling

Published in the United States of America

ISBN: 978-1-62746-623-3
1. Biography & Autobiography / General
2. Biography & Autobiography / Personal Memoirs
13.07.04

DEDICATION

This book is dedicated to my Dad who showed me loyalty, dedication, and honor with his life style.

To my Mom who showed me the importance of dreaming of what can be and determination to accomplish the dream.

To the tremendous Mother of our children, Janice, who believes in me and joins with me on our adventure in life. Thank you for all your love.

Contents

INTRODUCTION

In 1995, I had decided to leave a teaching position I had held for twenty-three years. That one decision set into motion an entire chain of events. That is how all decisions are, as Dad and Mom had taught me.

Janice, my wife of twenty-nine years, thought that we wanted to live in the south. As Providence would have it, the principal of a high school in South Carolina called. He had been conducting a national search for an experienced industrial technology teacher. After looking at my professional credentials and a background check, he had already concluded that I was his man before he had even made the call. Janice and I were both astounded at this event.

I moved to the south and started work. As time went on, I began to slip into a state of deep depression. The principal was a superb person to work for, and the school system was exceptional. I missed my wife who was also my best friend, my children Wade and Tawnya, and some lifelong friends. Janice stayed up north trying very hard to sell our home for three and a half months. We have a nice home but it never was sold. Thank God!

I was doing an excellent job of beating myself up while our finances and business were falling apart. I was at the very lowest part of my life. It was at this point that I began to write some true short stories about my childhood. The writing and the thought process caused me to arrest my emotional descent. I began to realize how influential and supportive Dad and Mom were to me, along with my friends and family. I actually began to feel the joy I had felt as a child through these writings.

I suddenly started to realize how often Providence would put just the right person in my life at the best moment—to put me back on the right path. I noticed that many of these people were part of the Greatest Generation, as it has become known. Dad and Mom were part of that generation. They were great teachers of life's principles without me knowing they were teaching. Their teaching was in the form of the life they lived. It has often seemed that these types of people have surrounded me. I did not know it at the time, of course, but it certainly became clear as I examined my life. I have concluded that none of this was a coincidence. I am so thankful that, most of the time, I had made the choice to listen to these great teachers.

I now know that all of us have people who come into our lives with a promise, but are we willing to listen? I hope that as you read these true short stories, you will be reminded of your own joys of growing up and the warmth of caring people, who, like angels, have stepped down from heaven for just a moment, with their message, to make life better for you and those you come in contact with.

And then, you too will become a seed planted and nurtured by this country's Greatest Generation. Their lessons are planted deep within us, and it is now our responsibility to plant for the next growth. Enjoy!

Love, Patience, Persistence, and Endurance

It was a very sunny spring morning. The sunlight was streaming through the bedroom window, followed by a gorgeous breeze. The spring air always smells so sweet and clean, it makes you want to get up out of your bed and not miss a moment of the day.

I got up from my bed and proceeded to walk to the bathroom in my loose-hanging Davey Crockett pajamas. I could hear the washing machine running as I approached the bathroom, where the machine was located. Mom always pulled the machine over to the edge of the bathtub when she was using it. The machine was always a curious device as it vibrated and danced through its operations. It was a real attraction in this beautiful morning. I approached the machine with great curiosity. I could see that the agitator was twisting the clothes back and forth. Next to it was a spin dry device which spun the clothes very fast to remove most of the water. Then Mom would take them out and hang them on a clothesline. This was my first close-up look at all of this machinery in action.

The wringer device produced the most attention-getting feat. The two hard rubber rollers were always rolling when the machine was running. Their job was to squeeze the water out of the clothes when you ran the clothes in between them. The rollers exerted a great amount of pressure against each other. Their white surfaces glistened in the sunlight as they turned. The soapy water produced the colors of the rainbow against their pure white surfaces. How could such a beautiful device be so harmful? I decided that it was not harmful because I saw *Felix the Cat* on the Saturday cartoons go through the rollers, and after coming out flattened, he blew on his thumb and inflated himself once again.

What could there be to fear? I decided to run my fingers across the bottom white roller as it squeezed the pretty shades of pink and blue, soapy water out over the perfectly white roller. I touched it very softly at first and then I ran my four fingers back and forth through the soapy sheet of water. My Davey Crockett pajama sleeves were now getting very wet and beginning to sag under the weight of the soaking water.

It was just a little part of the right sleeve that got caught between the two pure white rollers. The machine seemed to just grab that little piece of water-soaked fabric—it was as if it had teeth. The pure white rollers began to pull the pajamas in between the two rollers. I was now watching as the water was being squeezed from my pajamas. I was now pulling my hand back into the sleeve and up to the shoulder of the shirt. I knew that the cartoon cat was just a cartoon, and this was real life. In fact, it was my life. The pain was just too much for a little boy of four not to scream, as the white wringers finally got to my fingers and pulled them in as if it were a starved creature.

Mom heard that terrible and hopeless scream as she hung the clothes out on the line to dry. She knew by motherly intuition what was causing the scream as she ran for the bathroom. Once she was in the room, she did not say a word. She just went straight to work and hit the release lever, which released all pressure from the rollers. The rollers had already reached my elbow and had begun to roll up the flesh along with the pajama sleeve. It was a good thing a four-year-old child's arm is so small or more damage would have been done. I collapsed in Mom's arms as the rollers released their grip on my right arm, and then I blacked out. The next time I opened my eyes, I realized my head was in Mom's lap. We were in Dad's car—with him driving as a fast as he could to the doctor's office.

The next thing I remember is waking up on a cold, black table with a big, bright light up above me. The doctor was talking and putting some kind of green salve on my right arm. The doctor was telling my parents that the chance of me ever straightening that arm again was extremely slim. But my mom said, "He will!"

The next time I awoke, I was at home with my right arm in a sling and all bandaged up. Mom began explaining how we were going to work together on this project. I really did not know how serious the injury was. I was not worried, and of course, I believed Mom. God gives us wonderful gifts in our youth. The particular one I'm thinking of is how flexible we are to adversity in our youth. Mom didn't ever say that I had a severe injury or that the recovery wouldn't be complete. I just figured that everything would be all right.

Mom, as good mothers do, went right to work. She started saving the six-pack, cardboard cartons that Pepsi bottles came in. Cans were not available then. My arm would be in a sling for about six weeks, so Mom had time to prepare for her own rehab program. The doctor said that the bone was not broken, but the tendons and muscles were probably damaged. He thought the arm could not be completely straightened.

Mom's goal was to straighten and strengthen that right arm! Let the games begin.

The next six weeks seemed to fly by that spring, and Mom was ready. She was standing by the kitchen sink, pointing to the small, shiny, red tricycle when she said, "Take these empty six-pack cartons and load two at a time on the back of your tricycle. Then take them to the front door. Unload them there and come back and get two more." Once I had all ten at the front door, she instructed me to reload them and take them back to the kitchen door. She made sure that I did all of this with my right arm, of course. We would do this routine two to four times a day. The first time, it was very painful just to lift that empty carton. When Mom saw that it was no longer hurting, she put an empty bottle in each six-pack carton. It would hurt again, and she just said, "Good." It wasn't long that I had six empty bottles in each carton. I felt I was making progress because the arm was becoming straighter. That was when Mom began to fill the first bottle in the pack with water, and the pain started again. In a few weeks, all of the bottles were full—and my arm was completely straight. Mom's goal was to build up the muscles and have it be as straight as my left arm. Her goal was accomplished. She continued, up to this day, on telling me I could do anything I set my mind to do.

It was years before I knew what had been done to me physically and mentally. I participated in wrestling, baseball, football, basketball, and track—never even realizing that my mom saw me doing all these things and more in her mind, many years before.

Something Old, Something New

Times seemed to be much simpler in the early '50s except for the atomic bomb. I was thrilled to listen to the *Lone Ranger* on the radio, and then it happened. I went to Grandma's, where my aunts and uncles were all visiting. In there, was the first television in our family. This was the first one I had ever laid eyes on. It appeared to be just a wooden box with an eight-inch window that you could not see into. We all had to wait until dark to see what this window would show us. It was not that it had to be dark—it was just that programs did not start until six o'clock in the evening. I just did not know that was the real reason. I can just tell you that I did not want to wait.

To occupy my time, until the magical moment, I went outside on that very warm August night and caught some fireflies in a jar. I came back into the house and set the glowing jar on the table next to the wonder box. What a sight it was to behold when Aunt Aggie turned on that wonder box called a television. I really wondered if it would work, because it took a long time to warm up. You could count on the fireflies to blink on time. It was quite a sight in that room that night. Grandma, Mom and Dad, my sister, and my aunts and uncles—all of us basking in the blue light of that television and the yellow-green light of the dependable fireflies. The fireflies were always more reliable and more fun than the television as far as I was concerned.

It was remarkable how that television brought the entire family together for the evening. The gathering was always on Sundays. The dinner table would be whirling with conversation on what might be viewed that evening. What a change from the radio. The imagination is a personal and powerful thing, which was stimulated constantly by the radio. Now, you do not have to use your imagination—the screen gives you the image, not your brain.

One evening, we were all at home when Dad came home from work with a big box. My sister and I closed in on the box immediately because Dad never came home with surprises like this. He and Mom opened the box, and there it was, our very own television set. Our family life changed that very moment. Now, the entire family did not have to get together for that Sunday meal at Grandma's. All of the discussions and joy around what seemed to be an aircraft carrier-sized dining room table would be missed. We could now watch television from the comfort of our own little home.

Saturdays became much different. We could start the morning off with a good dose of the *Lone Ranger* followed by *Adventures of Wild Bill Hickcok* and then *The Roy Rogers Show*. Then we would get more current shows like *Sky King* and *Captain Midnight*. Sometimes, there would be a space show called *Flash Gordon*. This gave us fuel for our imaginations in the afternoon because we did not stay in the house—we went outside and played those characters out. Very often we made up our own stories and adventures. The fight was always for the good, and it was understood that the good guys always won. Sometimes, you had to be the bad guy because it was your turn. It was not so bad because once your character was killed, you could be the good guy again. It sure made you recognize who was who.

The toy weapon of choice was the Fanner Fifty. It was a six-shooter revolver that came with real leather holsters. It looked just like the one used in the *Lone Ranger* used. We all knew that real guns were extremely dangerous. Bobby's father was a hunter. We had no interest in messing with the real thing. Eliminating the bad guy and standing up for what was right and good in God's eyes was the goal. Protecting the good seemed to be what dominated our play. It all seemed so clear. As we all watched our favorite TV programs, we were influenced by characters that had very high standards. No one was ever killed in these programs. They were always wounded in the arm or leg. It was always assumed that the courts were sending them to jail for their bad deeds. We would kill the character off in our playing because we could not go through the court stuff. If the bad guy had been still around, we would not have been able to keep playing.

Sometimes, we would get together with some of our model planes. After we had assembled them, we would hold them in our hands and pretend we were flying them. We would then have these dogfights and be yelling at each other as if we were on the radios of the aircraft. It was always very exciting to be a pilot.

One day, I was flying my plane through my Dad's garden, all around the stalks of corn. It was a gorgeous, sunny day, and there were no clouds in the sky. For some unexplainable reason, I looked up in the sky: saw a flash and then a wisp of smoke. I wondered what it was. That evening my dad came home from work and told us that a B-47 Stratojet had exploded and then parts of it had fallen to the ground in the little town of North Collins. The evening news came on the TV and told of the crash, and then Dad said, "Let's go see if we can see it." We drove there and, sure enough, we saw a piece of wing and some other metal pieces on the ground. No metal struck anyone on the ground. I think the crew of two got out. This was a topic of discussion with my friends and me because now, flying could have other events besides being shot down. We later found out that the plane suffered from what was called metal fatigue. We had to find what that was, so we all were doing research to learn about it. This caused us to use the encyclopedia that Mom had purchased. A research frenzy, which any good teacher would have been delighted with, happened that summer. We found out that metal would actually become tired and break after repeated bending. This resulted in wing failure. It also caused me and my friends to admire air force pilots even more than we already did. The TV and the events around us caused us to be curious. The need to learn by looking into other sources of information, like the encyclopedia, became exciting research for all of us. We would learn more about other related areas, and then, it all became like a big adventure. Mom encouraged us to be curious. She loved to listen to our findings.

Joy in the Small Things

We definitely were not a financially rich family. Yet, it was realized by all of us that we had more than enough of all we ever really needed. The season of Christmas just seemed to magnify everything that was good in the life of this seven-year-old boy.

The small, cement block home we lived in had a fireplace and gas furnace right there in the living room. The windows were of the single pane, not the insulated variety which doesn't exist today. A most remarkable thing would happen upon these glass panes when it became very cold outside: it seemed to be the artwork of the angels, in the form of frost, right there before our eyes. The message they would write would never be the same as the message they had written the night before. This was made even more beautiful by the big-bulb Christmas lights that Mom and Dad had strung around the perimeter of those frosted windows. The frost would cause the beautiful glow of the red, green, blue, and white lights to fan out all over the panes of glass. A seven-year-old boy could spend a glorious time in a very special world of light from the trimmed windows and a very warm fire burning in the fireplace. The freshly waxed, black, asphalt tile on the living room floor would reflect all of those colors. The little living room became a room of wondrous warmth with colors that can only be seen again in your mind. When you became warm all over and with the smell the fire, it is so real forever.

The old, circular throw rug was a place to lay and watch the dancing light on the ceiling. This was all before the tree was brought in and set up. It was something how each year the lights just seemed to appear on the windows in late December. Who put them up there?

Dad came home from work one evening with a tree tied to the roof of his car. What an awesome sight—the king of my life with that giant tree on the roof of his 1946 black Buick! In 1953, a miracle happened because someone gave Dad the tree. Dad stood on the running board of that old Buick. With the fluffy snowflakes falling on him, he untied the rope holding the tree. They seemed to be two inches in diameter. My four-year-old sister and I were jumping up and down with great joy. Then, as he approached with this giant of a tree, we suddenly stopped. We both thought, *how is he going to get that into our house?* He then yelled for us to get out of the way. Mom held the door wide open, and somehow, he squeezed that tree through that front door. We were mesmerized at the sight of that tree standing inside our little house. The scent of that pine would forever be an imprint on my mind, as it wafted through the entire house. The smell was like a play button on a tape recorder. Every year, it brings back memories of family. The mind was one of God's greatest gifts.

Boxes came out of the attic and other places not known to the children of this house. They were full of lights and decorations and Christmas. Dad attached those lights. He would string those big bulbs on that giant, six-foot-tall tree. Once in a while, he would light up the house with his opinion of how the lights weren't working correctly, or they were in the wrong place on the tree. Mom told us to stay back so we would not step on any lightbulbs. Those strings of lights were all over that black tile floor, creating a constantly changing work of art. What a sight to behold! It was heaven in that little, warm, house with Mom, Dad, and my two sisters—and later, my brother.

We would sit on the sofa with our feet up. When we finally got the "Okay" to get down, we would go to the ornament boxes and pick one ornament to hold. Then, it was time to wait patiently while Mom decided where to strategically place every ornament on the tree. Sometimes, Dad would tell us where a particular ornament had to be put in a very special place. The truth is every ornament was very important. When they all came together on that tree, with the angel on top, the joy in this little boy was so complete—I would cry. That very moment was so warm, full of holiday smells, and the sounds of laughter. The colorful lights coming off the frosted glass added to the wonderful season. We were laughing in great joy because it just seemed that this time of year lasted for months. At least it was that way for us.

I could not wait to get home each school day to watch on our new television. It was only a half-hour show, but Santa was counting down the days to Christmas. He always had some kind of emergency to overcome to keep on schedule. Santa was an overcomer and a leader.

My Aunt Aggie worked at a department store in Buffalo, and Mom would take us there to that glorious place called downtown. It was so magical to walk on that snow-covered sidewalk and look into those gigantic plate glass windows. There would be displays to see of moving characters and new toys in action.

We had our own dream session surrounded by falling snow, the smell of hot chocolate and the corner vendor cooking hotdogs hung in the air. The colored lights were everywhere you looked. We listened to the ringing of the Salvation Army bells while we looked into those windows. Those same sidewalks were busy with people doing their shopping and walking quickly about four feet behind us—it was like we had an agreement. They gave us room to look in the windows, and we did not get in their way as they were completing their missions. And then came the great moment after about an hour of looking at the many displays. We went into the great department store to see Santa. We had been prepared by our time at the windows. My sisters and I were ready for the time to place our order with the big man. Just walking through the store was a joy as you looked up to see smiling faces. There were colored lights and gold trees surrounded by flowing cotton, which was supposed to look like snow. Gigantic Christmas bulbs hung from the ceiling, and they were dripped with the silvery, icicle decorations. Our ears could hear the Christmas songs throughout the store as we approached the line to see Santa. Once you talked to him, you got to go down a long slide right past the deer and snowman displays. Mom was there waiting with Dad, if he was not working.

"Now that our mission was complete, we headed for the car out in the snow-covered parking lot." We had a glorious ride to our warm, little home. The ride was made shorter by our conversation about what we had asked Santa for and on all the sights and sounds we had just experienced. My sisters and I were laughing and giggling with joy as we got out of Dad's car. We threw snowballs at each other as we walked to the front door of the house. Mom yelled, "Todge, stop throwing those snowballs at your sisters." They were laughing and squealing at the same time. It was such a joyous time to be alive. I know that God's angels had to be tickling us because there was so much laughter. Wow!

Grandma's House

Going to the local grandma's house was an adventure which I looked forward to with great anticipation. I say that it was local because my other grandma lived ninety miles away in the town of Palmyra, New York. In the fifties, ninety miles took about three hours to drive, but to a young boy, it seemed like forever. Anyhow, Grandma would always have some special kind of dessert treat fixed for presentation, and I was so appreciative of it.

Grandma was from Poland, and although she could not talk English very well, she did manage to communicate with me. It was like there was a sixth sense because she would say something in Polish, and I would have a general idea of what she meant. Then, I would answer her in English. As time went on, I would understand more and more of what she would say.

One day, while eating a very special, baked cinnamon apple that Grandma had prepared, this seven-year-old realized that I just might be on the verge of learning the Polish language. This was quite a thought for a young boy to have.

Grandma and I spent a lot of time together on warm summer days in her garden and around her yard, as she would prune, plant, and talk to her green children. It seemed like she had a direct line to God, as she made and told the plants what to do. One day, I observed her talking to the plants and the trees and even scolding the birds for nibbling on some cherries. This was a very normal event. I actually thought that this is what all Grandmas did.

There was no alarm clock at her house to wake me in the morning but there was something much better. Grandma would be in the kitchen before sunrise cooking and creating those magnificent scents, which would drift through the house like a river. I would be gently awakened by the scents of bacon and cinnamon bread. It made you wake up and follow the river upstream to its source. She never once woke me when she got out of that feather-filled bed that she slept in. It seemed to wrap right around you as you fell into it. She must have done that at the end of every day because she was always doing something. Even when she was sitting, she would be peeling potatoes or apples or some other preparation. I don't remember her ever being sick. It was as if she was to be perpetual.

At the front of her house, she had a sunroom that was full of plants that attested to Grandma's green thumb. She would have plants growing in the winter on that sunporch. The windows would be wet with the condensation on the panes of glass, but the room would be warm from the day's sun while winter lived outside. As the days grew shorter, they also grew colder and whiter. Inside Grandma's house, the smell of fresh-baked coffee cake and apple pie would drift at one level. When you stood on your toes, you could smell the fresh-baked bread higher up. It was a sea of pleasure for the sense of smell. Sometimes, the smells were so thick you could almost take a bite out of the air.

This was all leading to the festival we call Christmas. It was all I could do, just to keep from bursting with joy, as all of my senses told me that the time of celebration was approaching. The anticipation and preparation for the actual day would take wonder-filled weeks. This time was also a festival on that sunporch. The condensation on the windows would turn to frost as the calendar was closing in on Christmas day. The multi-colored lights suddenly would appear on those many small panes of glass. Their many colors would shine through the plants on that sunporch at night with rainbows of light around the outside of the shadows.

All this brilliant color on the frost-covered windows gave the room a complete and calming atmosphere, which could only be experienced at this time in this special and unique place. As the softly falling snow continued outside the window, it made me think that this is what it looked like when manna fell from the heavens. It made you feel like all was safe and you were taken care of. It was a comforting peace.

Stepping from the quietness of the sunporch through the door and into the festive dining room was like throwing open the canvas of a circus tent. There was joy in hearing the laughter and verbal banter of relatives who were just having a wonderful time together at the holiday. The room seemed to be brightly lit with the reflections off of the many shining faces. All of us grandchildren would think of games to play, and we would make up the rules and follow them or be banned from the games by the other participants. All of this play happened without adult supervision. The dining room table would seat ten people and always seemed to be the size of an aircraft carrier. It was only used at very special times of the year, or when there was an honored guest of the family. Otherwise, we would eat at the kitchen table. This was where the younger grandchildren would eventually eat on those special occasions because there was not enough room at the big table. The amount of food and the various kinds were always an adventure for the taste buds.

For me, the highlight of the meal was the desserts, which were usually coated liberally with whipped cream, a sugar icing, or a light coating of confectionary sugar. Some even had a coating of some type of cream cheese. The main courses were always the traditional ham and turkey, with all the fixings. Everyone would bring their favorite dish to pass, and if you brought something different or new, there was a great disappointment because we all looked forward to having those signature dishes. It was a family event of great magnitude, as far as I was concerned.

These festivities always seemed to occur at Thanksgiving, Easter, and of course, Christmas. And what made Christmas unique was what happened before the grand dinner.

We would always enter Grandma's house through the kitchen entrance. We were hit in the face immediately by the great smell of everyone's warming of the dishes and cooking of main courses. This was a preview of the coming attractions on that dining room table. We would take off our boots and leave them by the stove. We would collect all the coats, and it was my job to take our coats to the front bedroom. You could stand in that bedroom doorway and look straight through the dining room right into the living room. You could see the most awesome sight a young boy could ever see. I should have reminded myself that Christmas is about Jesus, but I didn't.

The magnificent sight in front of me mesmerized me. I had to get closer in order to make sure that my eyes were not deceiving me. As I walked past the huge table on my left and the glass windows of the sunroom on my right, I came to the entrance of the living room. Looking to the wall straight across from the entrance were gifts on the floor piled up against the wall, so high that my seven-year-old hand could not reach the top. It was a few years before I noticed that there was a couch under those gifts. The gifts were split up among ten grandchildren and ten adults. It didn't matter—it was still a remarkable display of God's grace and abundance in our family. It actually looked as if a giant slot had opened up in the ceiling above the couch. Then the presents just cascaded out of that slot, covering the couch and the floor.

The sight afterwards was almost as entertaining. We would make a pile of the wrapping paper and proceed to jump into it as if it were leaves in the fall. I would bury my sisters and cousins, and we would be giggling and become intoxicated in the sound and the moment of happiness. Then all the children would grab handfuls of the paper and take them to the old iron stove in the kitchen. This would consume the paper and, in the process, heat the tea and coffee we were about to have, with the mountains of Christmas cookies. There was a huge amount because everyone would bring three batches of their best cookies to the celebration. The kitchen would always be very warm from the stove and the excitement-generated heat from our bodies. The kitchen door would be propped open for a few minutes. We would get to see if the snow was going to make us stay later while we were cooled like air-conditioning on a July day. You just didn't want any of it to end.

Grandma would just sit and watch all of our activities and giggle at the sight of her many grandchildren. Soon, we all grew up and became teenagers, and the celebrations moved to our individual family homes. It was not the same for many years until it was time to repeat the process with our own children. I am so grateful to have such a great model to follow for our celebration years.

When Grandma died, it was a very different wake. I remember sitting around with the other grandchildren remembering the fun and funny experiences we each had with Grandma. We just kept laughing as we related our stories to each other. It had to be very odd to see so much joy at a funeral. That is what Grandma left us all with.

That is our inheritance from her. Thank you Grandma.

WHAT A DIFFERENCE A BIKE MAKES

The time had come for my very first bicycle. I knew this was the time because Dad said it was. That made it true. The people next door to my Grandma's house were willing to sell a twenty-inch bicycle for an extremely reasonable price, which Dad was able to buy. I did not know the brand name of the bike. It never entered my mind anyhow. I can tell you that it has a gorgeous, faded tan color with white stars placed at random on the front and back fenders. They were on the chain guard also. What really set this machine off were the two tan leather saddlebags on the back fender. I was in heaven because it reminded me of Roy Rogers's horse, Trigger. He was in golden tan color, with saddlebags, and he was a star. Let's ride!

I had never ridden a two-wheeled bike before, so Dad did something that I never expected. He removed those beautiful saddlebags. They just made the bike harder to balance for a new rider. He looked at me and said, "Come on," as he wheeled the bike across the grass to a small hill behind Grandma's house. He backed that bike up to a small pine tree at the corner of that big, white house. He said, "Get on." I managed to get on the seat myself, and it felt so big. That was when Dad gave me his one piece of advice. He said, "Don't stop peddling," as he immediately gave me a very strong shove down the grassy hill and over the backyard.

It was a glorious ride on a hot, summer day across a green carpet with the blue sky up above. It was so great to have the wind in my face and hair. It was great to move across the planet's surface faster than I could run. This was truly the greatest device for transportation of a young boy ever. Then it happened—the bike began to slow down because I was not peddling hard enough. I began to realize that it was going to tip over. I was preparing to dismount. The dismount would have been a two, if the Olympic committee graded it. The results were some grass stains and some brush burns. I made sure that the bike was all right. I ran with the bike back to the grassy hill where Dad was waiting. We did it all over again. By about the fourth run, I had learned to turn the bike and use the brakes. I was on my way to expanding my world.

At the end of the day, Dad put the bike in the trunk of the car and brought it home. I was exhausted and exhilarated at the same time. The bruises just reminded me of each run. I went farther and learned more on each of those launches made by Dad. Dad and Mom informed me that the bike was not to leave our yard until their permission was given. I did not even care because I knew that I had a lot to learn about this new steed before I tried to show off. I needed to work on my newly acquired skills. I just kept thinking that I have my very own first bicycle. Whoopee!

Sisterly Love

Time seems to drag so slowly when you are eleven years old. I think it is a good thing because you have more time to try and correct the bad decisions you made. I loved waking up to the gorgeous, sunny mornings of July. My sisters and I would have our pajamas on, as we would step from the backdoor of that tiny, cement block home. In our hands was a dish of watermelon for our breakfast. You had to pay attention to where you wanted to step. We were walking on the large rocks that Dad had placed inside a two-foot-high cement wall. Eventually, this would become an addition to the back of our home. This area was approximately ten foot by ten foot. It would be a few years before the cement would be poured over the large boulders which would act as reinforcements. Right now, it was an area where you would walk carefully. It was the perfect spot to sit in under the morning sun, eating a watermelon and spitting the seeds at my squealing sisters who would spit their seeds back at me. It was not a place to run around on. Mom would yell from inside the house for us to stop—we did, only when our watermelon was gone. It just seemed so great to be together in the sunshine, in our backyard, with the whole day of adventure ahead of each of us. I love my two sisters dearly.

The warmth of the July days would turn into very hot evenings. We would have the entire bedroom windows open to let in whatever breeze there was. We were usually in bed by nine thirty, as the sun slowly made its way below the horizon. It was time for the night games to begin. I would crawl out of my bed in the best imitation of a soldier that an eleven-year-old kid could muster—I was on a mission. The consequence, if caught, could result in painful punishment. I would crawl on my belly out of my bedroom to my door. I would then make an immediate turn to my left, which was the entrance to my sisters' bedroom. It was extremely important to be slow and quiet. The floors, which were made of rough planking, had a tendency to creak. Fortunately, my body weight was not that of an adult, and I knew which boards to avoid. A bigger challenge was to keep my giggling inside myself. My sister Anne would tell my sister Becky to lie in her crib very quietly so as not to attract the boogeyman. As I worked my way across the floor, Anne would tell Becky to move back against the wall and away from the raised bars of her crib. This prevented Becky from seeing me. Then she told Becky not to stick her feet out of the bars because the boogey man could bite off her toes. I could hear Becky's three-year-old body hit the wall, as she very quickly threw herself from harm's way. At the same time, I would be on the floor, rolling in silent laughter under Becky's crib. I had to do all I could to keep myself from laughing out loud. At the same time, I was excited about not being caught. Anne would tell Becky not to move because boogey was now under her bed. At that instant, I would grab the springs under the mattress of her crib and then pull them down with a snap. Then Mom would yell from downstairs and tell us to stop. The excitement was almost too much to contain. Becky would squeal, and Anne would immediately tell her to be quiet or the boogeyman could get real nasty. Becky would get real quiet. Now, I would put my feet up against the springs and give her a bounce. Becky would scream out and then be very quiet. Mom would yell that if we did not go to sleep, she was going to send Dad up. We all knew what that meant. Pain!

Becky eventually got fed up with this monster coming into their bedroom that summer. One night, she just stuck her foot out through the bars of her crib. When she was not bitten, she slid over to the edge of her crib and got a look at the boogeyman under her bed. She looked me right in the eye and smiled. She screamed to Mom that there was a monster under her bed, and she could not sleep. You know the rest of the story. She did have the last laugh. Anne just watched the whole thing from her box seat at this event. And that was the end of the boogeyman.

Even though there was unspoken but healthy love between a brother and a sister, there were still things that were off limits to my sisters—like our clubhouse in the woods. This was something very important to a boy who had turned thirteen. Anne wanted to get into that clubhouse in the worst way. To this day, I still do not understand why. One day, she met me about halfway to the clubhouse. I was walking home, and she was walking towards the clubhouse. She demanded that I bring her to the clubhouse and take her inside. When I answered her with a no, she grabbed my cap pistol from my holster and ran to a large apple tree and climbed right up. She climbed to a point where I knew the tree could not support two of us without the branches breaking. She held the cap pistol as a hostage and proceeded to yell down her demands. She held it out for about ten minutes when, in her frustration, she threw the gun down at me. Anne was a very accurate thrower because she hit the top of my head with the pistol. I fell to the ground, stunned by the impact. As I moved to stand up on my feet, I felt a lump on top of my head. As I pulled my hand down, I could feel wetness. There was blood on my hand. Not anything severe but just the right amount to send Mom over the edge when she came looking for us. She asked what happened, and I told her that Anne threw my gun down at me from high up in the tree. Anne was still up there. She knew she was going to get it. As her feet hit the ground, she was running for the house as fast as she could. Mom had come looking for us because she had been calling us for a while. When she did not get an answer, she came looking for us with her weapon of choice: a dreaded, black, hard rubber flyswatter. The hard rubber end was attached to a very thick wire handle. Mom could wheel back and, with the perfect wrist action of a professional, flick the end of that fly swatter so it would come off with terrific velocity. Mom could hit a fly at twenty feet with this thing—we were easy targets.

Mom was angry with both of us when she first approached, so I just held out my hand. She saw the blood, and I knew I was home free. Anne knew as she came down the tree that she had to be fast. Mom got her with a couple of swats to the behind. I was grinning as I took a slow jog toward our home about thirty-feet ahead of Mom. Then I heard her yell, "You need to answer me when I call for you or tell me where you are going. You're not off the hook with me smart guy." At that very instant, the hard rubber end of the dreaded flyswatter caught me squarely and painfully in the behind. Mom explained that there would be more coming when we got in the house. I would always tell her where I was going after that. I also knew that if I made a wrong choice, there would be no working my way around the consequences. There were no time outs in the game of life. We always looked out for each other when the chips were down. We knew that is the way Dad and Mom wanted it to be.

Time marched on, and we all became a little older. One afternoon, Mom was out grocery shopping. Anne, Becky, and I were home alone. We would play games with each other, and this time, it evolved into wrestling on the floor of the living room. This went on for quite a while. My sisters then realized that the two of them together could do a job on me. I decided I had to get the upper hand. I had to get out from under these two who had managed to almost pin me to the floor. As I worked my way out from under them, I grabbed Becky's feet as I stood up. We had been wrestling in the center of a round rug, which was made up of braided pieces of cloth. These braids were then sewn together end to end and wound around to form concentric circles which were all sewn together. As I stood up with Becky's feet in my hands, I looked down at her while we were all laughing and giggling. I stepped back and off of the circular rug and was pulling Becky's feet toward me. She was facedown, and I wondered why she kept raising her head just an inch off the rug as I was pulling. At the same time, I could barely hear her muffled yelling. Then I noticed that it was Becky yelling but her mouth was shut. About the same time I noticed that as I was pulling on her, the braided rug was moving right along with her. I dropped her feet and ran to her head to see tears rolling down her cheeks. As she lifted her head about an inch, I could see that her new braces had become tangled in the threads of the rug. She moved herself forward just a little and was released from their grip. Immediately, she threw her head back and screamed. "You jerk, that really hurt." Then she on jumped me and started punching me, but we all fell to the floor laughing at how she looked. Those threads hanging out of her mouth were a real sight. I stopped laughing just long enough to go get some scissors so we could trim her mouth. Anne made sure we got all the threads trimmed before Mom got home. As we were trimming, we would just start giggling at the sight of all our fingers in Becky's tiny mouth. I know that episode did more to straighten her teeth than any doctor could do.

Mom got home and noticed the rug had moved. She looked right at Becky's red face and zoomed in for a look. We had missed one little piece of thread. How do moms do that? We had to tell her what had happened. Even Becky was laughing.

None of us ever wanted to hurt each other, but I can tell you that there were no more wrestling matches. We were all growing older and bigger. Most of all, we loved each other. Our lives were now developing beyond horseplay. Mom made sure we knew it.

CHURCH BOY

Faith was becoming an important part of my life, but I did not even realize it was happening. Sunday mornings always seemed to be the sunniest. Mom would always call my name breaking the beautiful silence of I was sleeping in. She would stand by the side of the stairs and yell at the top of her voice—at least it seemed that way—for me to get up. I knew that I would do as she had requested. All the while, I was mumbling bad things about having to get up when the sheets had finally reached the perfect temperature. I proceeded to get dressed in my best clothes, go down stairs, and meet my sisters who were ready to leave for church. We could have gone out the front door, go across the road, walk about two thousand feet through the field, and be at the backdoor of the church. That would have been a great way to get there even if it would have been a little messy on our good clothes. Instead, Mom drove us around the block to the little church.

It was always much better after we got there, at least in my mind, because I did not want to go. My sisters did not mind it at all. We would get out of the car, walk up those front steps, and I would see my friends. Anne and Becky would see their friends too. We would then go our own ways as we entered the sanctuary. We very seldom sat together unless Mom was with us. It always seemed like there were two hundred people but maybe one hundred was a closer number. The short church service would end, and we would then go to our assigned class areas in the back of the church. As you went through the door to the right of the platform, you would enter a large room which was divided up by the placement of chairs in various circles in the room. Each circle represented a different age group, so as you grew older, you would move to a different age group and a different circle of chairs. Each circle of chairs sat on its own piece of circular carpet. The goal was to get into the class in the balcony, which was where the teenagers had their class.

We used the Bible extensively for all lessons and were not given someone's interpretation of what it meant. We learned that it simply means what it says. This resulted to having a very firm foundation for the rest of my life. I realized when I was around ten years old that Dad would go to mass at seven in the morning before any of us were awake. He would faithfully go every Sunday. You see, Dad was Catholic, and Mom was a Baptist, so that was why we went to a congregational church.

When our classes were all done, we would go back into the sanctuary for some more singing and then dismissed. As were walking out into the sunlight, we would be looking for the car. It would never show up. This was summer time in the '50s. We were safe to walk home, and Mom knew it. I would be grumbling on how she would make us go to church while she would not go. Then she would leave us and forget about us. I was just having my own pity party as I walked home with my sisters. They never seemed to want to join my party. They would just be looking at the trees and the flowers that were blooming. This would bring me out of my bunk and back to the joy of the moment. When we would arrive at our home and walk in that front door, the smell of bacon, eggs and toast would hit our nostrils like an avalanche. This would overwhelm all of our previous thoughts. The sight of the toast piled high on a plate with the jelly and honey running off from it and then down onto the plate was overwhelming. You could taste all of it, long before you put it into your mouth. Sundays really were very special, as we all came together for breakfast—and as with most special moments, you did not know it was special until many years later.

As the years passed, the time we spent walking home together turned out to be a great time for us to learn about each other. We would talk about school, our friends, and whatever was happening in our lives at that time. The sight of my father cooking breakfast would always be a very comforting sight when we reached home again. We knew it was Sunday because Dad was laughing and cooking breakfast. The upper half of the front horse door was open, and the Son filled our little home with so much joy. Mom would always remind us of that very fact. Dad would always respond by a simple nod of his head. All was right in our world.

The Dogs of My Youth

When you are twelve years old, a dog can have an effect on your life—most of the time it is a good effect. In my case, it was two beagles that started a chain of events involving man's best friend. Their names were Lucky and Tippy. They spent most of their time in a dog pen made of chicken wire. The pen was about ten feet wide and twenty feet long. The doghouse was built right in the center of pen. The dogs would eat their food in the front yard of their house and make their deposits in the backyard of their house. It was a good, clean system. It was a beautiful July day, and everyone was very excited about the Fourth of July celebration. We all had our fireworks, and we were ready to set them off when we could.

One day, I brought a firecracker with me to conduct an experiment in the dog pen. I entered the dog pen, and as always, I closed the gate behind me. When Lucky and Tippy heard the gate, they ran to greet me with wagging tails. I knelt down to pet the dogs. I noticed that the week's deposits behind the doghouse were all in a very neat pile. It was a large pile.

I did not smoke but Dad sure did, so it was very easy to get one of his cigarettes, break it in half, and use it for an extension of the fuse on a firecracker. This would give more time to escape the explosion. I slid the cigarette down onto the fuse. When it was lit, it would give another five minutes of time, as the heat would eventually ignite the actual fuse, which would then burn very fast.

I took the explosive with the cigarette on the fuse and inserted it into a selected pile. It went in deeper than I thought, so only the cigarette was showing. Lucky and Tippy were interested in this project that they were sniffing and looking at my every move—very closely. The moment that I struck that match and lit that cigarette sticking out of that pile, they both suddenly stood at attention. It was as if they had a vision of what was about to happen. That match started a whole chain of events along with the chemical reaction. The dogs stayed at attention for, maybe, two seconds. You could almost see their pupils dilate, and the adrenalin start to flow in their bodies. They both exploded into action. Their legs were running, and the stones were flying in every direction. They were trying to get traction in the gravel in the dog pen. When they did get traction, they seemed to move at the speed of light right past the doghouse. When making the turn to go into the house, stones from their flying paws were bouncing off of the house, hitting me. The two of them then were trying to get into the door of the doghouse at the same time. Once they were in, they would not even stick a nose out. I was right behind them. I was now at the front of the doghouse so that the house was between the pile and me. The fuse was taking longer than I had anticipated. I was yelling to my friend Bobby. These were his father's hunting dogs. Bobby finally came and opened the pen door and entered.

As he closed the door, he turned to look to see where I was. I knew the fuse must be lit. Already, my imagination gave me visions of what could happen. It was all I could do to keep from laughing, as my mind had completed the event. Now, real time had to catch up. I stuck my head out from the protection of the house to see where Bobby was and at that very instant the device went off. As intended! A hard piece of manure flew and hit me right between the eyes. This almost knocked me unconscious. The only thing which kept me awake was the screaming of Bobby.

I managed to stand up and see a sight that very few will ever witness. Bobby was standing straight up with his arms sticking straight out from his sides. He had a coating of different shades of brown, covering him on the front and absolutely nothing but clean clothes on his backside. It was just like the sunlight hitting the moon. One side is covered with light, and the other side is completely dark. The difference was the color of pink when Bobby opened his mouth to scream, and the whiteness of his eyes when he opened them. He walked very slowly and stiffly to the gate of the dog pen, as if he were a robot. That was when Bobby's mother came on the scene, responding to his screaming. As her eyes scanned her son, she gasped and stuttered for him to stand still while she began to tell me what she thought of me. She was right and I knew it. She kept on yelling while she got a bucket of water and a sponge. I could have just walked away, but I knew she was a very kind person, and no matter how funny I thought this all was, she deserved my respect. I actually felt bad because of the labor I was putting her through. I also knew that when my Mom and Dad heard of this incident, there would be a punishment given out. This would result in being grounded, along with a good, old-fashioned spanking.

I started to walk home after Bobby's mother told me to go home. I could not help but relive the event and have a good, deep laugh. It was one of the few times in life when the actual event matched perfectly with the imagination. I did not have a motive to hurt anyone physically. When I reached my home, I found that Bobby's mother had not even called my parents. In fact, I don't think my parents even heard of this until I told them years later. Bobby never treated me as if he was mad at me. We remained friends. I guess everything came out in the wash.

Dogs would continue to be a factor into the following summer. I was thirteen that summer, and it seemed that they really were dog days filled with swimming, baseball, water balloons, and a lot of bike riding. I loved to ride my bike everywhere. I polished, washed, and maintained it because I bought it with my paper route money.

One day, Tom and I decided to take a good ride. Tom and I had become very good friends. In fact, we are lifelong friends—up to this day. Our time together was special even back then. We decided to wash our bikes. When we were finished, we wanted to take them for a spin to dry them off. We liked to watch them sparkle in the morning sun. We wanted to go down this road which had a very steep hill on it. This would serve to blow off the water on our bikes and cool us off at the same time. We crested the hill and started down.

We decided that this would be a great time to see what kind of top speed we could get out of these rigs. Just then, we both realized that two dogs were barking up a storm, as they were coming after us. They had chosen the wrong angle to intercept us. With our increasing speed, they had to change their direction. At this point, their path resembled an arc. These dogs were in trouble, and none of us knew it until one of them ran straight into a steel pipe holding a mailbox. The sound of his head hitting that pipe had a resounding, pinging noise.

Tom and I looked at each other in total disbelief of what had just happened. We burst into uncontrollable laughter to the point that it was hard to control our bikes. Then, an even more astounding thing happened. The second dog kept on his mission and wound up about two feet in front of both of our front tires. He was astounded also. You could see it in his confusion. What made it worse for him was that we were still accelerating. He would turn to the left and bark at my front wheel, and then he would turn to the right and bark at Tom's front wheel. At the same time, we were gaining on him. He was running on total confusion, because now, the two front wheels of our bikes were right next to him. Our laughter suddenly turned to concern because we both knew what his next move was going to be. The wind was blowing in our ears. We had to yell at each other to communicate. I said, "He is going to turn into one of our front wheels. He was not going to stop. He has nowhere else to go." We continued our laughter, and then it happened. That dog suddenly turned to the right and ran straight into the front wheel of Tom's bike. The impact caused the bike to turn to the right and forced Tom off the road and into a ditch. He was bouncing all over but managed to stay on the bike. I remember talking to myself and saying, "Stay up on that bike, ride it baby." Then I could see where he was heading. He made it up on the grass and out of the ditch. He was heading right for a fire hydrant and a telephone pole, which had a space between them of only three feet. Tom was still traveling at a very high rate of speed. If he put the brakes on, he would lose control and slide on the grass, right into those two very solid objects. I shouted, "Put it right in between them." Tom's eyes were clearly focused on the task at hand. His bike was bouncing all over, and yet he put it right in between that pole and the hydrant. I knew in my heart that a guiding hand was upon him and that bike.

We slowed our bikes down, pulled them to the side of the road and laid them on the grass. We ran two or three steps and fell to the ground, laughing together and reliving the entire episode. We were catching our breath and pausing in wonder that we were both safe and unhurt by all of this. We lay on that grass and looked up at the blue sky. We both said, almost in unison, what a wonderful day it was. We looked at each other, grinned, and said, "Let's do it again." We got on our bikes and rode to the very top of the hill, turned, and came blasting down it again. As we came to the spot where the dogs were, we were astounded to see those two dogs just sitting at the end of the driveway. They just watched as we rode by. It looked as if they were saying to each other, "We have learned our lesson, but you two haven't, so we're going to watch you."

What really hit us as we were riding slowly home was that through all of this, those two dogs were not harmed and neither were we. The angels were all around us—protecting us. We learned you could not have the exact same experience twice. So learn to enjoy each day because you only that moment once around.

THE PRINCIPLE OF ICE CREAM

Motivation is always an excellent tool when enforced in a positive way. Mom knew how to motivate me. She wanted me to do the dishes after supper each night. This was not something very exciting to a twelve-year-old boy. Supper was an experience at our house. Mom would yell out that supper was ready. We would come to our small kitchen and sit down around our brand new, red, oval kitchen table. It had chromed steel legs and matching red vinyl-covered chromed steel chairs. I almost always sat at the end of the table with my back against the wall, with the side of the refrigerator to my left. It was so close that I could reach out my left hand and touch the fridge. My sisters were sitting to my left along the straight edge of the table which was sticking straight out into the kitchen. Mom sat on the other end of the table in the middle of the kitchen with my Dad to my right. Mom was on the end because she was working the kitchen counter and the table. It was a very practical arrangement. For me, it was a strategic arrangement.

The first time we had broccoli with our supper, this became very apparent. Dad was not always at supper because he worked two jobs. This gave Mom the opportunity to experiment with new foods or dishes to serve. Broccoli falls under the heading of new foods. We were not excited about this new food. Suddenly, I had a brilliant idea in that light green kitchen with the red furniture. I could eat some of the broccoli and throw the rest behind the refrigerator. Thankfully, Mom would only give us a small serving of this new food. The first time that I made my move, I thought that my sister Anne's eyes were going to come out of her head, but she remained silent and acted as if nothing had happened. I was amazed at her silence until we had supper the next night. She ran to the table when supper was announced and sat in my seat—under a very small protest from me. I suddenly realized her strategy. The new food for that night was fried burdocks from the field behind our house. I know because I was the one that Mom sent out to pick them. Anne knew it was her turn to use the magic refrigerator trick. The other part of the deal was the person sitting in the bonus seat had to sweep the floor after dinner. This was the only way that Mom would not find the evidence of our tactics. This was understood among all participants. Becky was far enough away from the seat that she never got a look at our activities. That cover was blown when Anne told Becky what was going on. They were going to sleep one night when the secret was told. I found out she knew when, one evening, she was sitting in the bonus seat after about six months of our covert actions. Spider, as my Dad called her because of her long legs, did not know about the clean-up duties that went with the bonus seat. She almost blew our cover to Mom by not volunteering to sweep the floor after dinner. Anne jumped in and volunteered. She let Spider know that this could not happen again. It did not. Mom did not know for years about our pact, and the special chair it involved. She just thought it was wonderful that we cleaned up after supper. We did not volunteer to clean when she was not experimenting on us. The code of silence was never broken until we had all graduated and had moved out of the house.

One night, Dad was home for supper. We knew that when Dad was home we were not going to have any experimental foods to broaden our taste. We all made sure that we did not snack before supper because supper would be a good, old-fashioned mashed potatoes and meat. This would include a very common vegetable, like corn or string beans. Mom announced that supper was ready, and we all went and washed our hands. I made sure that I had a decent shirt on because Dad and Mom liked it to look like a decent place to eat. Dad gave the blessing, and we began to pass the food and fill our plates with all of this real food. It smelled so good, and we all knew that Mom was a good cook, especially when it came to the basic food groups. We must have looked like starved rats eating for the first time in weeks because Mom told us to slow down. She then told us to save some room, because tonight—we have ice cream for dessert. I did what she said, and then I asked a dumb question in my excitement. I asked what flavor of ice cream it was. My Dad put down his fork and said, "You are not having any ice cream." I asked why, and Dad said, "If you have to ask what flavor, you do not want it bad enough." And I did not have ice cream that night. I thought that Dad was being mean.

A few days later, Dad explained while he and I were riding in the car. He had seen starvation in India and said that ice cream in most other counties of the world did not even exist. It was a luxury. The ice cream also represented his work for our family, and although he did not take it personally, my asking what flavor really did indicate that I was taking it for granted. Dad just wanted me to know what a privilege it was to live in this country. He told me that it was an everyday occurrence in our lives, but we need not take it for granted because it is not like this everywhere. Dad's experience overseas made an imprint on his life. He did the same to us in so many ways, but we did not realize it at the time.

Enjoy Where You Are!

Sitting in that classroom in late December was a tremendous challenge to a twelve-year-old boy. We all kept looking out the huge school windows for those magnificent white snowflakes. They had to come from the angel's hair that Mom was going to put on the tree when we got home from school. The school was always very warm and those huge, eight-foot-tall windows were all steamed up. They were just waiting for our masterful marks to be put on them with our fingertips. The footprints across the windows were fun to make, but eventually, you had to erase the easel so you could see outside and give the weather report to your friends. The report came with accuracy. It was wonderful to hear and actually witness. The snow was falling so heavily that it seemed to be blocking out the bright afternoon daylight. A boy certainly didn't think of the traffic problems the snow might be causing, except that there would not be much traffic by his house. Yes, the roads would be ours on this night out.

As we all headed for our school buses, we were so excited to see our breath. It was great to be alive in this downfall of white powder. On the way to the bus, we ducked a few snowballs and then lined up to get on for the trip home. The ride was actually the time to set up appointments, meetings, and assign groups for the afternoon and after-dinner tournaments. I stepped off the bus and began the short walk to my house. I knew that once I got inside the door of that warm, cozy, little house, the smell of the fireplace would just warm my very soul. Home was identified by all the senses. Two combinations told me, I was home: the fireplace burning, and the smell of freshly baked bread.

Then Mom did it. She handed me the shovel. All she said was, "Your father needs to get into the driveway." I knew I would be late for my appointments and meetings. That driveway was just gravel, so we didn't want to shovel it down to the dirt. The shovel was actually an old, rusty, coal shovel. Were we discouraged? We had people to meet and things to do. The first thing to do was to make sure we left a good, hard snowpack and get this minor delay over with. Sometimes, a friend might help, but no matter what, the job had to get done.

It was after dark that we seemed to be at our best in this white wonderland. We knew that the highway department was thinking of these kinds of evenings because they had strategically placed a telephone pole with a light on it by the end of our driveway. We thought this was for our night games. You just turn left leaving our driveway, and you go right under our streetlight. As you continue down the street forty yards, you come to the top of the hill on our street. There was very little salt used on the roads at that time so the side roads kept their icy white covering much longer. The snow falling gently under that streetlight was an invitation to fun. This setting—along with your steel runner sled and three or four friends—meant it was time to run. We each carried our sleds with both hands, and in unison at the crest of that hill (our hill), we would all start running. On some inaudible signal, we would belly flop on our sleds at the same time.

The goal was to see who could go the fastest and the farthest. This required keeping your sled on a straight path. You had to be very precise in your steering and be smooth in all of your movements. The only sound you could hear was the sound of cold, hard, highly waxed, well-maintained steel runners, hissing as they slipped across the ice-covered road surface. It was that beautiful hissing sound which became much louder if you had to make a correction in the course you were on. You could easily tell who the most skillful drivers were by listening to their steel runners talking in their own language of speed. I had inherited a good, soft touch from my father. At least, that's what I thought. So I knew that I would win the most of the time. A good night on the hill would result in fifteen to twenty good runs. The last three would almost always result in laughing and talking about why we were not fast on that night.

When the road was not completely ice-covered, we would resort to a game of full contact sledding. This involved the practice of swerving over towards your friend's sled and grabbing the side of his sled while he was trying to do the same thing to you. The victory was when you got a good hold of his sled and flipped him off it while avoiding the bare spots of pavement. The real champion learned how to hang on to the sled after flipping the opponent and take his sled down the run with him. Your opponent would then have to walk to the end of the run to get his sled. Sometimes, two of us would be grabbing each other; and concentrating so much on the goal, we would both wreck into the most glorious explosion of white, soft powder, entwined with our sleds and each other in the ditch. We would burst into laughter at the imagined sight of the wreck. We would replay the event with our own verbal videotape.

Building snow forts and hiding in the fifteen-foot-tall evergreens that were along the road next to our streetlight was an excellent arrangement. We would wait for a person to walk under the streetlight and throw a snowball way up into the dark sky. The thrower couldn't even see the snowball once it went up above that street light The snowball would then make its arching decent down to earth where it hit its intended target. The whole event was very exciting to see because of the skill it took to estimate where the target would be. The intended target was always unaware of what was coming down on them. The fact that three to five of us would launch at the same time meant that five snowballs were coming down out of the darkness ever so quietly. The target would have an astounded look on his face when he saw and heard that first snowball hit the ice-covered road. Instinct always told the target to run, and then, the other four or five snowballs would come smashing down on him and, hopefully, hit him. After all, that was the goal. This actually became a science project. One had to learn about speed, trajectory, timing and, most of all, the judgment of where the target would be running. Teamwork was also needed in all the games we devised. If you broke our rules, you didn't participate. The laughter and friendship created an atmosphere which could only lead to one outcome—success.

Wondrous thoughts of what we would do tomorrow and talk of what we had done yesterday caused many people to want to be a part of what we had. We didn't really know how wonderful it was on those gentle nights filled with snowflakes on our tongues. A slow walk home to the warmth and love of our little homes awaited us. The winter was never cold to us. Winter was hot and sweaty with the constant movement, laughter, and friends having fun together.

LIFE IN THE HALLWAY

The flexibility of a child is truly an awesome thing, and it should be carried on into adulthood. I was about twelve years old when my grandmother (my mom's mother) came to stay during August one summer. This was a big change for me because Grandma would sleep in my room. We lived in a very small house of about seven hundred square feet. This was for four children and two adults. We just knew it as our home and really never thought of it as very small at the time.

We had a living room, a kitchen, Mom and Dad's bedroom, and a bathroom on the first floor, with a hallway between the bedroom and bathroom. This hallway led to the narrow stairway and the two bedrooms upstairs. As you entered the hallway from the living room, an immediate right or left would put you in Dad's bedroom or the bathroom. If you continued down the hallway for another eight feet, you would hit the staircase which led upstairs. The total width of the hallway was about six feet. There was also a desk against one wall in this hallway. When Grandma came, we would set up a cot in the hallway, and this would become my bedroom. It was just something that we did, and we all knew it was out of necessity.

This one particular year, Grandma stayed past Christmas. To this day, I don't know if there was a special reason. In fact, I think she stayed until spring. It was very memorable for all the right reasons.

The hallway was a high traffic area, and this meant that it was a great place to harass my two sisters as they went off to bed or to the bathroom. The downside was that they could return the favor after I went to sleep. This changed as time went on, and the novelty of the situation wore off. Everyone had to go by me sooner or later, since I was right next to the bathroom. Having only one bathroom in a house with seven people added to the business of this one area of the house. What made this time so memorable was Christmas of that year. Family in that little house became so important at that time of year.

I remembered Christmas morning because my sisters awakened me as they came down the stairway whispering very loudly to wake up or be jumped on from the stairs. This was entirely possible because there was no railing in the stairway. I had to wait for my sisters to go into the living room anyhow, so it was not a big deal to be awakened by them. I threw the covers off and put on my slippers. We were all so excited to come out of that hallway and see the beautiful tree. I plugged in the lights and just hoped that one of those lights was not burned out. The whole string would be out if one of them was out. Mom would use angel hair and a few icicles on the tree. The lights would just glisten off of them. It was dawn outside, so we plugged in the window lights also. We just wanted all the lights on—for this was such a special time together, and we knew it. It was also time to light the fireplace to give the room some heat. The living room floor was made of black, asphalt tile. This would absorb the heat from the fireplace and glisten with a reflection when it was freshly waxed. I worked at keeping it that way by washing and waxing it for Mom. The lights played a tune of glory across the frosted panes of glass and onto the angel hair which was spellbinding to a child. Add to that the smell of the fireplace and the giggles of the family—we thought we had just a pinch of heaven in our home.

It was the last, small gift which turned out to be extremely special that year. My sister Anne, pulled this small package out from under the tree and said, "What is this? It is very heavy for its size." She then said that it was for me and brought it over to me. She laid it on my lap. I proceeded to open the gift and was very shocked to find a small transistor radio. These were very expensive in 1958. I was one of the first of my friends to have such a device. I think I carried that radio with me everywhere over that Christmas vacation and ran its battery down in the first few days. I remember going to bed holding it to my ear and quietly listening to it as I lay on that cot in the hallway. I was feeling so fortunate and blessed, as I was taken away to other places and listened to faraway stations.

It certainly did not matter where my bed was as long as I was in my home. Living and sleeping in the hallway never harmed who I was or am or how much my parents and sisters loved me. It was a good thing there were no social workers around us then.

ANY BALL GAME WILL DO

B aseball was the first sport to really capture my attention. During the long glorious summers, it seemed like there was a game somewhere in town every day. I decided to play with only certain individuals like Dave, Bob and Lenny. We would play with three people and the batter in Bob's backyard. The rules were that there would be a pitcher, two outfielders, and a batter. The field was of shale stone, so we didn't do much sliding. The batter would have to run to first base and back home to score a run. When he had three outs, the batter would then rotate to the outfield while an outfielder would then pitch. The former pitcher would now become the batter. A complete rotation would be called an inning. After a designated amount of innings, we would figure each person's amount of runs, and he would be the winner of that game. There was a rosebush hedge along the edge of Bob's property, and all of them were full of thorns. If you hit the ball over that hedge, it was considered a home run. We usually played until someone had to go home. This meant that one game could take hours. The small area of the backyard allowed us to play with only four people where a regular ball diamond would just be too big of an area to cover. We would always have funny things occur, and thus, we would need a rules interpretation. We were our own rules committee. We all learned the art of negotiation and how to work with others for a mutual benefit.

One such incident was a result of frustration, but it caused a lasting rule change to affect our little game forever. Dave had hit a nice, fastline drive to his right of center field. Bob finally got the ball out from under the rosebushes. It was not over the bushes, so it was still in play. He then picked it up and threw it to me. I now had to make a decision. Out of frustration, I took the ball and threw it at Dave as he rounded first base and headed back to home plate. The softball hit him very solidly in the back. No one knows if it was the force of the throw or the shock of the incident, but Dave went down on the ground. I then declared that Dave was out because I had hit him with the ball. Dave was crying when he got up off the ground and declared that he was going to quit playing. This somehow supported our idea that he was out. Thus, it became a good rule. That was until I came up to bat. Suddenly, I realized how foolish this new rule was, but it was the rule. This meant that every hit was for the home run fence, or you were playing dodge baseball. At first, this was great fun, but it very quickly lost its appeal. We returned to the original rules we had laid down because every time you threw the ball at the runner and missed, he would score.

Baseball was our summer staple, but as we became a little older, baseball would share just a little time with football. Football had very simple rules in our neighborhood. Stop the guy carrying the football. The playing field was the front yard of Bob's house. This was because, unlike the backyard, the front yard was all grass. Sometimes, two-hand touch would be played, and if we were all feeling tough that day, we would play tackle. The main hazard was that one end zone was the famous rosebush hedge, and the other was a stone driveway. When anyone scored on the rosebush end, he would pay a very thorny price. One particular incident stands out in my mind. I had broken away and was on my way to a very certain touchdown on the rosebush end of the field. I was actually running away from the herd of opposition when it hit me on the top of the head. I had just reached the rosebushes for the score when the stone hit. I could not believe that someone would do such a thing. I was in pain and instantly became extremely angry. I turned around and faced those other players to see who had done this. I immediately started running back toward them—screaming in anger and ready to punch out every last one of these cowards. Bob and the boys had a dazed look on their faces and backed way off to stay clear of the roundhouse punches I was throwing. They thought they were witnessing their first mental case. Through all the anger, I reached up to touch the top of my head for the blood that was surely there from that stone. As I pulled down my hand in front of my face, I was shocked to see the thick, dark purple fluid all over my hand. In unison, all of us looked up to the sky to see a gigantic flock of birds flying over our heads. Every one of my friends fell to the ground immediately and began rolling around in great laughter. I began to laugh too, and then, I began to cringe in disgust at the thought of what was upon my head. That game was done for the day. Now I knew why real football players wear helmets.

THE KITE AND THE SNAKE

Summer is always a glorious time to be outside and to be dreaming of things to do and places to see. This summer was very warm with a fantastic breeze off of Lake Erie, which was about two miles from my home. For some reason, I never realized how close this grand sight was until I was a teenager.

The cool of the morning always would lead to the heat of the day. This cycle would produce a soft breeze that would have a sweet smell to it that would last until early evening. This was the perfect time to fly a kite. The breeze was warm, and the sky was a gorgeous sight with all the reds, pinks, blues, and puffy white clouds. The grass would bend over ever so slightly in the breeze and actually look like waves in the ocean. You could see the beautiful pine trees dancing with one another in a back-and-forth motion. This often seemed like a stage show. The maples and willows seemed to hear an altogether different song and did an altogether different dance.

All of these sights and sounds sent a very exciting message that said, "Go get the ball of string and tie it to the kite." It was time to go out and catch the elusive breeze that would now cause my kite to dance. I took the kite from Dad's garage and tied the end of string from the ball to the main center string on the kite. As I walked out of the garage, I could hear, feel, and see the music of the wind begin to play on the kite. The dark blue, tissue-thin paper would snap to tightness and pull on the string as the breeze caught it. The paper refused to tear. It was almost as if the kite was saying, "Let me go, now!" The paper would continue to snap and crack its orders in the breeze. I walked through Dad's garden to the small woods and onto the open field behind my home.

This field had no trees, but it did have some ditches and a couple of two-foot-high anthills, which would be of concern when launch time came. I made a mental note of where all of these hazards were and plotted my course for the launching run. I stood very still to feel which way the wind was blowing. As I stood there, the breeze ruffled through my blonde hair, and the fragrance of the field grass and the field flowers filled my nose with a glorious aroma. The scents never leave your brain. When you smell them again, you think of the warmth of summer, home, and a relaxed time of life. God lets you replay it over and over for your joy.

The paper snapped and tugged at my hand as if to remind me of why we were here. The kite was telling me with each tug, "It's time, and it's time now." As we ran across the field, the kite took flight in just three steps. It seemed to leap into the air with the skinny little string keeping it from its total freedom. There were thin, white strips of torn bedsheet used as a tail to stabilize the kite in the wind. What a sight to behold. The dark blue kite began to dance as if it was standing on a white leg, and the sight of all this against the light blues and pinks and reds of the evening sky could take your breath away. Looking up at the one hundred yards of curving string made you forget any cares you may have had that day.

As I continued to very slowly let out more string, I didn't remember the small bush I must have stepped into with my right leg. I kept my concentration on the kite, but I noticed that the pressure of the branches from the bush was increasing around my leg. That certainly did not make any sense. I stepped back to get out of the bush, but the pressure was now moving slowly up my leg. I decided to look down at my leg. Then terror went through my entire body at what I saw. It was not a branch of a tree or bush. It had a white body with black blotches. To me, it looked like the fabled anaconda wrapped around my right leg in two coils. Suddenly, there was only one thought. Get this thing off of me right now! The adrenalin must have been flowing so hard that it smelled. All I know is that I could have kicked an eighty-yard field goal with the force of the kick that sent that two-foot-long snake flying off my leg and spinning through the air. The sprint back to my yard must have been at world-record speed. As I stood in that backyard and calmed down, I knew that no one was going to understand what had just occurred, and then it hit me. I had forgotten about the warmth of the sun, the breeze, and my kite. I walked back to the scene and saw the ball of string on the ground about twenty feet past the site of the incident. My senses were now on high alert to everything around me. I slowly picked up the ball of string and followed it to the grounded kite.

The paper kite snapped its paper in the breeze as I lifted it off the ground, and I knew right then that there would be more kite flying in this field because we had beaten the chicken snake. The kite spoke louder of the joys to come, the smells of the field, and the sights of the sunsets. When I got home and went in the house, I told Dad about the snake. He very calmly asked if I had kicked it off. Since I answered yes, he just gave his approving nod, and our lives all continued on.

MONOPOLY BY STORM

One glorious Christmas, we received a game of Monopoly. We would play it once in a while, but it just seemed too complicated to keep our interest. Then a big snowstorm hit our little town, and our attitudes changed. The roads were not plowed or salted. Actually, they were rarely salted, so when the time came to learn to drive, it was on the snow and ice-covered roads. We just learned to sled on them. We knew we were in heaven because we were not having school. We would be outside playing in the white fluff all day. We would make snow fortresses, which had many chambers or rooms, and then, we would modify them just because we could. There was really no one who would attack our forts except for my sisters who had to inspect our work. We changed our forts, just so they would not become familiar with our layouts. This was very important to twelve-year-old kids.

We were also required to shovel out the driveway, which, at the time, would lead to a snow-filled road. As long as the road remained unplowed, we could take breaks from the driveway and have snowball fights. When that plow came through, it made us angry and happy at the same time. We knew the plow driver was happy because we could see him laughing when he passed by our pristine driveway. We would stand at the end of the driveway, and he would throw the snow up into our just completed work. The laughing just added to it. Then we would look at the shiny surface that the plow revealed and got to work, cleaning the plow's mess so we could go sledding. What a sight at night to see the moon glisten on that icy surface. The moonlight reflecting on the snow would just light up the road for our night games. Night or day, the reaction was the same. The long shadows caused by the sunlight would produce rainbows in the snow and sometimes, even revealed the different colors of the snow. Sometimes, it was light blue, and sometimes, it was pink. Being outside was always a new adventure, but we were always grateful to return to our warm homes.

The fireplace was roaring with fresh wood, and supper was done. The excitement was at a fever pitch because Dad and Mom were going to play Monopoly. Even as we were setting up the game, we knew that this was a very special time. The entire family of Dad, Mom, Anne, Becky, and I were gathered around the table for an evening of family fun.

The card table was set up right in front of the fireplace. The sight of that room was dazzling with the light from the fireplace reflecting off of the black tile floors, and the heat being absorbed into those black floors keeping your feet so cozy. The game went on well until after midnight, and it was a barnburner. We would each become heated with the emotion of the deals. We had dis-covered the pace of the game.

We could hear the wind howling outside, and we would all let out a cheer as the weather became worse. We took a bathroom break, and Dad walked over to the front door and took a look outside. We all ran over to get a look and could just barely see the streetlight at the end of our driveway. We could see that the snow was really drifting across the unplowed road. It was Thursday, and school was already cancelled for the next day. We all thought that we would play all night, but Dad knew we would not last. Mom said to leave the game setup, and we would pick up where we left off the next day. We had never played a game where it would last for days. This game was very exciting.

When we awoke the next day, Dad could not get out to work because the roads were drifted over. Dad never missed work. Suddenly, while we were listening to the radio, the siren at the volunteer fire hall started blowing. Dad, being a volunteer fireman, had to leave. Someone in a snowplow picked him up. We later found out that Route 20 had been shut down because a tractor-trailer had rolled over on that highway which passed by our town. Many people were taking refuge from the storm at the fire hall. Mom was a member of the Ladies Auxiliary, so she got a phone call to go over to the fire hall. They needed people to make sandwiches for those stranded at the fire hall and for the firemen working the emergency calls. Someone picked up Mom in a snowplow. She said that I was in charge and that I was not to leave my sisters for anything. We could see the back of the fire hall from our house because it was across the field and on the other side of the block.

The game continued as we bought up Dad and Mom's properties in an auction style. We had great fun arguing about it, but we worked it out. We were really developing our bargaining skills. Mom came home after serving lunch to the stranded people and gave us a description of what was going on. She stated how grateful the people were. I thought that I was grateful to be warm and fed as I went out to the woodpile for more wood for the fireplace. We were wheeling and dealing in the game when Dad got back and told us about the trucks and cars that were stuck all over Route 20. He said a total of ten vehicles were stranded on the road. That was a lot for our area, since there was not a lot of traffic under normal conditions. Dad gave me a box, and when I opened it, I saw a pair of green rubber boots. The type of boot that was high-cut with the laces at the top of the boot. I immediately put them on. Dad said that each of the firemen got a pair from the trucker whose rig had overturned. I guess he was grateful for their help. Those boots meant that the only wetness my feet would ever feel again was that of my own sweat. I could now stay outside for as long as I wanted instead of having to come in when my feet got cold. Dad said that when you put those on, always put two pair of socks on so the pair closest to your skin absorbs the sweat from your feet. It was like he could read my mind. Now, I could really work that snow. Right after I had that thought, Dad said I could shovel the driveway without coming in to warm up my feet. He got this big grin as he turned away and said, "Let's make a pizza." We began to work the dough and then stopped to let it rise when Dad said, "Let's start a new game so your mother and I can play again." The current game was two days old. My sisters and I had a two-second meeting and said yes because this would be the second time in two days that we were all playing together. Dad did not have to go to work at either of his two jobs, so it was a yippee day. The next day was Saturday, so we had another two days of tournament Monopoly. What great fun crying and laughing and learning about money.

The seasons always change, and life goes on, but we were still into the game when the warm, spring rains came. This also meant that we would have thunderstorms, and sometimes, we lose power. One night, at about five o'clock, a thunderstorm hit, and it knocked out our power. We all looked at each other, and without a word being said, our training went into effect. We all got great, big grins as we went to work. I went out to the woodpile and got wood for the fireplace while Anne and Becky were finding and lighting all the candles anyone would ever need. I was getting a great fire going when all of us noticed Dad standing at the front door with a camera in his hand. He was staring out the front door with a look of astonishment on his face. It was dusk, and as we approached his back, we were all struck with silence and wonder at the glorious sight. The sun was setting behind our home and sending its golden rays of light in front of our home, turning the trees to an amber color. The lawn and the tall field grass in the field across the street were a golden color also. The sky was a gray-black color behind all this gold. Among all of this gold was our little, glowing, white church. The church was about three hundred yards straight across the field from us. Out of those dark clouds came the arch of a brilliant rainbow. As you followed the arch of colors that were so intense down to the ground, it was as if the arch was going right inside of the glowing, white church. It seemed that our collective breath was taken away at that very moment. It was as if we were being told out loud that God was protecting us. Dad lifted the camera and took a picture. He stood there silently for a few minutes more, as the revealing sun went behind our home. He turned and said very softly that more rain is coming, and it may be a very thunderous night. We played Monopoly all that night and only noticed the storm in the background because we were not afraid. We rested and picked it up again the next day. That night, the storm had left. As we ate supper, we bragged on how we had made our deals in the game as we enjoyed the warmth and protection of our cement block home and our family. God himself told us it was so!

THE BLACK BOX IN MY ROOM

The summer before I entered the eighth grade was a very melodic time in my life. My friend Doug had introduced me to music on the radio in 1955, but it just did not interest me at that time. Time marches on. Your life prepares you for your next steps if you let it. It just seemed that the music was now telling me a very important story. Actually, I was ready to listen. I remember wondering how someone could get very excited about some song on the radio. Now, I had become one of those people.

At first, I was just caught up by a pretty melody or a very catchy tune. This made sense to me because Dad always said that intelligent people would listen to symphonic music. I knew that Dad was right. Mom would back him up, so I just figured that symphonic music was the only real music, and that was the end of it. That, of course, changed when I started listening to the radio.

The sun was high in the sky on a July morning in 1959, and I decided to put the windows of Dad's 1955 Ford Station Wagon down and enjoy the car radio for just a few minutes. It was about eleven o'clock in the morning. The next thing I knew, an hour had passed by. I was immediately enchanted by the announcers and fell in love with an instrumental recording called "Because They're Young." It was a very natural thing to like this type of music first because I had been used to hearing symphonic music. I was so enchanted that I saved my money and went out and bought my very first 45 rpm record of that song. It was the only record I had. I played it over and over in my Dad's garage. He was not in the garage at the time, of course. I would spend much of my time listening to the radio and did not realize I was almost becoming addicted to this music. I think Mom and Dad knew I was infatuated with this thing. Mom decided to give me this old 1947 radio. It was all black in color and about twelve inches long and twelve inches high and about six inches in depth. It had a very large dial for tuning in the stations. The dial was about four inches in diameter. The dial was black with small white numbers on it. It would whistle, howl, and hum when you first turned it on because it had tubes. These had to warm up for you to get the station to come in. It was almost like the radio was telling you to back off and let it warm up before you ask it to do any work. A small knob that was about one inch in diameter controlled the volume. I always made sure that the volume was turned down when I turned it off in my bedroom. If I had not done this, the radio would be screaming at everyone in the house the next time I turned it on. It was a very loud complainer if you did not treat it respectfully.

This black box of sound was left at my command. In my room, I utilized it extensively. As the sun would set, I would go to my desk in my room, turn on my light, and then turn on my radio. I allowed the black box about ten minutes of warm up time and then, ever so slightly and slowly, turned up the volume. Then, it would be time to tune it to my favorite station: KB. Some of the songs would be very mellow or sad. Others would be so joyous you could almost do cartwheels to them. As the temperature dropped outside, and the days grew shorter, I would spend more time in my room listening to songs and the stories they told. The disc jockeys would sometimes tell a story in order to introduce a song. It seemed as if he was looking right into my life. I would hear a song and think of the girl I liked at the time. If only I could just say those words to her like the song did. Another song would be how I felt about her. This was not the only thing I thought of because there were other things in my life. I just knew I was not spending as much of my time building snow forts anymore. I guess I was getting involved with life.

The seasons changed. The snow would bring Christmas songs and all the joy I have always felt at that time of year. The songs just seemed to make your body warm and your heart tingle. One Saturday between Thanksgiving and Christmas, I was washing the black, asphalt tile floor in the living room for my Mom. I was just getting ready to put some wax on the floor, and I was actually excited about this. I knew how glorious it would all look reflecting the fireplace and lights. There was love on every face that walked in that front horse door—as we called it. You could open the top half of the door and leave the bottom half closed. It was unique and gave visual security but still let the outdoors into the room. I had the top half of the horse door open as the first snow of the season was falling with those giant, one-inch flakes against a backdrop of clouds and, sometimes, blue sky. The sun would go in and out of the snow-filled clouds and present rainbows of color across the black tile floor. Mom and my sisters were out, and Dad was working that morning. I had just finished applying the wax to the second half of the floor. I would do one half of the floor, and after that, I would dry the other half so you could still walk through the living room during the waxing procedure.

I was standing at the horse door watching the snowfall, and the song "Jingle Bell Rock" came on. I was enjoying that song so much that I started dancing. As I jumped and spun around, the joy of the season just kept building in my heart. I thought I would burst like a balloon. As the song came to an end, I jumped up and slapped the wall above the arch leading to the kitchen. I felt a very sharp pain in my index finger as I pulled my hand down from that archway. I stood there and saw the source of the pain. A pin was sticking completely through my finger and out the other side. It just missed the bone on the way through. There was only one way to get it out—so I grabbed it and pulled it all the way out the other side of my finger. I ran the finger under the cold water from the faucet. I thought, *What is a two-inch-long needle doing up there?* The song "Sleigh Ride" interrupted that very thought. Nothing would stop me from enjoying the music and feeling joyous. The news came on, followed by the weather report, and the announcement that it would be a white Christmas. I never did find out what that needle was doing up there, but that weather report was exactly what the doctor ordered.

That evening, I went to my room and turned on the black box. I went back downstairs as I waited for the black box to warm up. As I entered the living room, the fireplace glowed in that freshly waxed floor, and I could feel the warmth coming right off that black floor. The colored lights in the windows on each side of the fireplace and the large flakes falling outside caused me to think that if this is so warm and wonderful, what must heaven be like? I slowly turned, soaking up the entire atmosphere, and returned to my room.

As I entered my room, I could see and hear a passenger train coming through on the tracks, which were about a half-mile across an open field from my house. Those people were going somewhere, and so was I—as I turned up the volume on the black box. The news was on, and although it was mostly local, the national news would always take you on a journey. We never thought of the national news having an effect on our lives but that started to change. The music would come back on. The words were starting to mean a lot, and the black box would set a mood in my room. The words to the music were for someone special in my life. Who would that someone special be, and what would she look like?

OH! TO READ

I t was the best of times and the best of time. We did not always realize that it was a great time to be alive. After all we were in eighth grade, the girls were looking pretty good, and I had a best friend named Tom. Life was becoming very exciting. Every great adventure was full of surprises. This was my own fault because, sometimes, I would do something goofy and not really know why. Sometimes, it would work out good, and sometimes, it would not. I just stopped thinking that far ahead—it was like I would have a short circuit in my brain. I guess that's what eighth grade is all about.

One day, we were taking a midterm exam in history class from Mrs. Bockmier. She was a tall, thin lady with thinning red hair. She always stood very straight and had an elegant way about her. It just seemed like the normal thing to do was to respect her. She was at the end of her career, but she clearly loved what she was doing. We loved her back. We just did not say those words.

My desk was moved right up against the blackboard in the front of the room. Mrs. Bockmier had assigned me that seat for some strange reason. If I turned my head to the left, Mrs. Bockmier's desk was about six feet away. The chalk tray was directly in front of me and in it sat a three-foot-long eraser. It was as if this object had a voice because it kept getting my attention while I was taking my exam. In fact, as I wrote my answers with my right hand, I could caress that eraser with my left. Then I would answer its call by sliding it back and forth in the chalk tray ever so slightly and slowly. This action was meant to cause the eraser to pick up as much chalk dust as possible. I wanted it saturated with the white dust. My right hand had finished the task of the test, but the left hand was working even harder at its task. I put my pen down and began to giggle to myself as my mind was already in the fast-forward mode. I was imagining what was going to happen next. I could see it all as plain as day. The great part was that I could replay it over and over again in my mind. I started laughing even more. I was enjoying this so much that I wanted everyone else to share in my joy. So I made one of those eighth-grade decisions based strictly on the flow of the juices of emotion. I knew I had to make this come to life so that all of my friends could enjoy this too.

Without even thinking of the consequences, I picked up that three-foot-long, chalk-soaked eraser. As I held it in my hand for only an instant, Mrs. Bockmier's words—in which she had leaned over and spoke to me one minute before—rang in my ears. She said, "I am stepping out of the room for only two minutes, so behave, you are taking a test." I knew I had only one minute, and I could see Tom sitting there right next to the door that Mrs. Bockmier had walked out of. The door was at the very back of the room. The temptation was just overwhelming. I let that three-foot-long eraser fly. I had seen it wrap around Tom's head in a cloud of chalk dust. It fell to the floor leaving a white chalk ring around Tom's head. That is what caused me to giggle earlier. In real life, the eraser did hit him in the head with a magnificent explosion of white powder and a lot of coughing on Tom's part. However, it did not wrap around his head but just fell to the floor leaving a pile of dust on the floor. As the eraser bounced on the floor twice, it seemed to stand on end for an instant just as Mrs. Bockmier walked in the door. It was standing at attention for her, and then, it just quietly fell over at her feet. She very quietly looked down at it. Then she bent down and carefully picked it up. Her eyes immediately went to the front of the room. I sat at the front of that room in disbelief on how this had all played out. I knew I was done, and I would receive my just reward from Mom when I got home. Mrs. Bockmier came to the front of the room. She carefully placed the eraser in the chalk tray behind her desk. Her lips were tightly stretched across her face as she stared at me. She slowly approached me, leaned over and asked very softly, "Did you get out of your seat while I was gone?" I said, "No." She knew I would not lie. She nodded and turned and sat down at her desk.

I was astounded at my stupidity and at Mrs. Bockmier's understanding. She proceeded to collect the test papers and continued her classroom procedures of having us slide our desks back into the neat rows. When we were done, she called me to her desk at the end of the period. She asked if I read very much when I was at home or away from the school. I told her that I read comic books about the army or World War II books. She then asked me if I liked trains, and I answered yes. She reached out to her bookshelf and pulled down a big, two-inch-thick book on the history of the railroads in America. I thanked her and took the heavy book home with me.

When I got home, I began to look at the pictures and found them very interesting as I read the captions under the pictures. A few days later, I decided to start reading the text of the book to find a deeper understanding of the pictures. I had been hooked by the wonder of the pictures and did not even realize it. I proceeded to devour the book over the next month, looking and then reading, and reading and then looking. This was becoming great fun. I learned that Westinghouse invented air brakes. Then I found out that B. F. Goodrich lived thirty miles from my house, as did George Pullman. Pullman invented the sleeper railroad car. I was on a whole new adventure in this book, and then it started to overflow into other books. This "reading thing" was very addictive.

Then one day when I was in Mrs. Bockmier's class, an astounding thing happened. She asked the class who invented the air brake. There was silence in the room. I knew I was the only one who knew the answer, and I did. What great fun it was to have everyone turn around with a where-did-that-come-from look as I smugly sat there realizing that reading does have its rewards.

I suddenly felt that I was not stupid or slow. Nobody ever said those words to me—I just felt that everyone was much smarter. It was a revelation to find out they were not. I began to go to the library in the school just for fun. I would read a magazine or scan the history area for a book that sounded interesting to check out. I actually started to read the magazine articles instead of just looking at the pictures. I began to realize that by reading and feeding my mind, I could imagine far more than any television program or picture book could show me. My mind was becoming a projection screen for whatever I would feed it through reading. Who could design such a device to do such a miracle? I could hit the replay button of my mind as often as I wanted to and enjoy it all over again.

I have been a reader ever since because Mrs. Bockmier entered my life, and she was the first teacher to truly hit the record button of my mind. She was placed there for a purpose, and I am grateful!

My Fishing Father

Fishing has become a great relaxation, but it was not always that way. Dad loved to fish, and at first, I could not understand why. Then he got me involved. Dad awakened me at five-thirty in the morning and away we went out to the door. When the cold air hit me in the face, my brain said, "You are crazy to freeze and be up at this hour." My heart knew I was doing this to be with my Dad.

As father and son, we drove to the Niagara River and then subjected ourselves to a wet, cold day. We just wanted to play with sharp hooks, cold, wet fishing line, and dripping water all over us. Just touching the sides of the aluminum fishing boat would send a chill through your entire body. Then the tackle box would give this shriek scream as you moved it across the aluminum boat hull. It just seemed that your entire body was constantly being assaulted by these irritating sensations. Then, when you caught a fish, you would have all this cold, smelly slime all over your hands from handling the fish. The only thing that would clean it off was the cold water from the Niagara River. How could anyone call this relaxing?

We would hook into a fish, and none of these irritants mattered anymore. The thrill of that creature fighting to get away, and then pulling him in—not really knowing what kind of fish it was—turned out to be extremely exciting. This answered why Dad loved fishing so much. This was his relaxation.

His favorite fishing was for musky or northern pike. Dad would take his eight-foot-long rod and unreel about eight feet of line. He would then snap a steel leader, which was about three feet long on the end of his braded line. This was all in preparation for the big lure that was to be attached. This lure was made of wood with two hinged joints. This would allow the lure to wiggle like a fish as it was pulled through the water. Dad would get the boat moving just a shade above, stay idle, and then drop the big lure over to the side and into the water. The instant that the big-jointed lure hit the water, it began to have a swimming action like a real fish as it was being pulled through the water by the boat. Dad would then start letting the line out very slowly until the lure was about sixty to a hundred yards behind the boat. He would then take the rod and set it in this special rack or holding device. He would then concentrate on the tip of the rod to see if he had a fish on the line. Dad knew where all the weed beds were. He would steer the boat so that the lure would take a path right along the edge of those various weed beds—which was where the big muskies lived.

When a big Musky would attack the lure, it would bend the rod, and the vibration on the tip of the rod would stop. This was the signal for Dad to take the rod out of its holder and then give the rod a big jerk. This was done to make sure that at least one of the three treble hooks would be set into the fish's mouth somewhere. Dad said that, sometimes, the big, old, smart fish would take the lure and play with it the way a cat plays with a mouse. In other words, they were treating the lure like it was a real fish. So that was why Dad would give the strong jerk to the rod.

When Dad hooked into the first musky with me in the boat, it was exciting and shocking at the same time. As he reeled that fish up close to the boat, I was astounded at how big it was. It was about thirty-six inches in length. When it opened its mouth, I must have jumped back at the sight of all those teeth. I remember seeing the teeth of a barracuda in pictures, and that was what the musky's teeth looked like to me. It was the nastiest mouth I had ever seen on a living creature. I grabbed the net and scooped that big fish up tail first. I lifted him out of the water and into the boat. Everything was okay until I lowered that fish into the boat. It seemed to explode with movement the moment that its body touched the inside of that boat. The fish was flipping very violently and seemed to jump three feet straight up. As it did, the exposed hooks were flying around. Those teeth were looking sharper as that fish was snapping for its very life. In an instant, Dad stepped on that fish and proceeded to wack it on the head with a baseball bat until he was sure it was dead. He then explained to me that this was the only way we would be safe in the boat, as he pointed to the fish's mouth. He did not wear gloves when he would handle a live one. This always astounded me because he had never been bit or wounded by the teeth. I was not prepared for what I was to witness when we got home.

When we got home, Dad went to the backyard and laid a newspaper across a wood table. He then lifted the fish out of a water-soaked paper and threw it up on the table. He then took out a long, razor-sharp knife and cut open the fish's belly to see what the fish had been eating. I did not know at the time that he would always go through this same process with every fish he caught. I thought he was just being curious. He wanted to see what the fish had been eating so he could use the bait they wanted next time out. Sometimes, the fish's belly would be full. They were not hitting the lure because they were hungry. He said that the lure just did something they did not like, or they might be protecting a nest that's why they hit the lure in anger. This generated much interest from my mom and my sisters and really caused us to look forward to the cleaning of the fish. This was what it was called in order to get the meat which we enjoyed eating.

One morning, Dad and I were fishing on the Georgian Bay in Canada. This was a magnificent place to do anything outdoors during summer. We were fishing in a bay we called "Deep Bay."

You could look across the dark blue water of the bay to the shoreline where there was a stand of white birch trees. They looked as if they were standing at attention in the glacier-carved bay. Behind them were beautiful pine trees. The clear blue sky and the very bright sun of that morning, combined with the magnificent reflection of the pines and birches in the clear blue water, made you know you were in His picture. Even with all this beauty around, the fish were not biting on my lure.

A few seagulls were flying around, and in boredom, I said to my Dad that I could cast straight up and hook a seagull. He laughed and said, "That will be the day." Dad did not know how much time I had spent in the backyard casting at various targets for distance and accuracy. I was prepared for the challenge. I picked out an incoming gull and took aim on where I figured the gull would be in his flight. With a snap of the wrist, the tip of the rod bent under the tension of the casting movement, and then, the tip snapped forward as if to throw the lure out all by itself. The lure was released. Its mission was just like a missile in flight. The line followed the lure upward and glistened in the sun with the colors of the rainbow as the line chased after the bird.

Then, remarkably, the lure found its target and hit the gull right under the right wing. The gull was shocked, and so was my Dad. It was instinct that told me to set the hook. The gull came down to the water, and I reeled it in like any other catch. Dad was really laughing, and so was I, as the catch came closer to the boat. It came to the back of the boat as I reeled it in. That was where Dad always sat in the boat. He reached down to grab the gull, and it took hold of the back of Dad's hand. It did not release his flesh from its beak. Dad finally was able to unhook the bird with his other hand. The bird had to be pried loose from his hand. I was about ready to take a screwdriver and pry that bird's beak apart to get it off of my Dad's hand. When it finally let go, and both of them were released from each other, that bird just sat on the surface of the water looking dumbfounded but virtually unharmed.

As we drifted away from the bird, we just laughed and laughed. What a great time together. Fishing was the only time when Dad was truly relaxed. He loved being outside, and he loved it even more when he could see that his children loved it too.

We went out again the next day and caught six northern pikes in one hour. They were very tasty at supper that night. Now, I was the one that was hooked on fishing. The cold, slimy fish smell disappeared, and the time with Dad doing his favorite hobby was what counted.

Track is the Ticket

Running is a big part of any young boy's life because he is running from something or to something. In my case, it was to something. In fact, I know now that God used it to steer me towards my assignment in life.

I played baseball with my friends from the age of eight up to high school. At that time, I knew I could outrun my friends in a foot race. I just never equated that with speed. I could always run them down in a short race of, say, two hundred yards or so.

It was puzzling that none of the physical education teachers ever saw that speed, except for one. I loved baseball, so it seemed very natural for me to go out for the baseball team as a freshman in high school. The coach thought I should play first base. I was disappointed as a sophomore. I just thought I should have played more. I think that is a very common thought in most good athletes. I did not complain or talk to the other players about any of this because—that was not what you did on a team.

In the spring of my junior year, I went out for the baseball team again. We were in the spring training sessions, and one day, our practice was cut short because of rain. I was walking to the team room when I noticed the track team doing some starts on the tennis courts. They practiced in the rain. After questioning what exactly they were doing, I learned they were sprinters. They were practicing coming out of the starting blocks. This one very tall and confident fellow came over to me with a swagger and said,

"You want to try this?" Then I said, "Sure." He then proceeded to instruct me on how to get into these starting block things. He was very patient and kind to me. He continued to explain the starting procedure and sequence of words involved in the start of a race. I realized that this was far more complicated than I thought. I was very surprised at the amount of thinking that was involved. You had to be sharp at all times. Dennis, which was my instructor, then asked if I wanted to try a start. I answered, "This is really neat, let's try it." I watched everything that Dennis did to get into his blocks right next to me. I did the same. A fellow sprinter gave the commands of set and clapped his hands. We both took off for about sixty yards across the tennis courts. I had beat Dennis. A very strange silence fell over the tennis court as we walked back to the starting blocks. Dennis became very silent, and I thought I had done something very wrong. I broke the silence when I asked him if I could try it again. There was only a nod of his head in a "yes" manner. I thought that maybe he was very tired. We ran again, and we had the same results. As we were walking back the second time, the track coach had just arrived. He said, "Do you want to try it again?" So we did, and it was a tie. The coach just walked up to me and said, "You need to switch to track." I thought that I had just had a great time, and my mind was made up as I was walking to the team room. When I got inside, some of the guys on the baseball team had been watching all that transpired and informed me that some of the guys on the track team ran to get the track coach to watch me run against Dennis. They said, "You beat him! Do you know who Dennis is?" I answered, "No." They said that he was the best sprinter in Western New York. I was completely shocked. I really was in disbelief myself, and that I had not experienced this. Then the coach came into the team room and asked me if I had decided to run track. I said, "I think so." He answered, "Good, because you just beat the best around here—twice." Now, I suddenly realized why about twenty guys were so quiet on the tennis courts that day.

I experienced immediate success on the track as the season progressed. I started to believe I was a good athlete. That summer, some members of the track team decided to form a summer track club to compete in Summer Olympic development meets. These were track meets where you would actually compete against Olympians in training on a handicap basis. As you became better, your handicap would decrease. As an example, you may start five yards ahead in a hundred-yard race, and as your time got better, your handicap was decreased. The goal was to start alongside the Olympians and be in the race for a spot on the team. It was very heavy stuff to think about having your shot. This also put me in line for the junior Olympics in our town and the county. I won the hundred-yard dash for our town. I proceeded to the county meet where you would run against the best from the city of Buffalo. I won there also.

All of these experiences led to a relationship with an official who was observing my actions and performance as a person and as an athlete. I first came in contact with Mr. Ambrose at a high school track meet in the village of East Aurora. He took me aside and instructed me on how I was practicing my starts to his cadence illegally. He calmly told me he had to disqualify me if I continued. I did not argue but chose to remain silent and responded to him with a "Yes, sir." A bit later, he walked over and explained how I could practice the starts legally. I really appreciated his advice and thought how wonderful it was because he could be just like the others and not take the time from his duties. He just smiled and then walked away. I saw Mr. Ambrose again at the Olympic development meets that summer and at the Junior Olympic meets. He stated that he had been watching my name in the paper, and my running was progressing nicely. I thanked him and was surprised and honored that he noticed. He then proceeded to do his job as always. The winners at the Junior Olympics received medals and trophies, and during the winners' ceremony, Mr. Ambrose was a presenter. He presented me with the gold medal for the event. He then informed me that they were short of trophies, and I would not be getting one. I was disappointed, but I knew that was just how it was. I just responded with an "Okay!" Mr. Ambrose knew how to make disappointment disappear. About three weeks later, I was jogging down the street where I lived, and a car passed by me. I saw the brake lights come on as it was now in front of me. The vehicle proceeded to back up to where I was. I thought that he was probably lost and wanted directions. The car stopped next to me and in front of the pine trees, which offered such great protection and joy for our winter games. I looked into the car at the same time the driver turned to look at me. My spirit jumped because it was Mr. Ambrose. I was sure he could see my surprise when I said his name. He put his car in park and said, "Ted, is this the street you live on?" I answered, "Yes sir!" He responded with, "This is a beautiful place to grow up." He turned his head away from me, and when he turned back, he said, "I have something that is yours." He lifted two beautiful gold-plated trophies through his car window and presented them to me. They were the trophies for the Junior Olympic victors. He just stated that he knew they were important to a champion. I was astonished, and I thanked him. He never left the seat of his car, and I can still remember the warmth of his smile and the glint in his eyes because he seemed to be as thrilled as I was. He proceeded to put his car in gear and said, "Ted, keep running son because it will take you somewhere!" He started to leave just as I thanked him again. I just stood on the road as he drove away. I looked down at the trophies in my hands and thought this man had to find out where I lived. Then he had to drive twenty-five miles, one way, to deliver these to an unknown sixteen-year-old boy. This was a very special kind of man in my life. It was like he was an angel sent to nudge and guide me in the right way. His words were very prophetic. I continued running in my senior year of high school, and I also was a sprinter in the Summer Olympic development meets.

There are decisions that change your life. Dad had heard that there were some openings in the tool and die apprentice program at the local Ford plant. I went down, applied, and went through the process of testing and interviewing, and to my father's amazement and mine, I was accepted. This made Dad very happy.

I continued to participate in the track meets that summer, and it was at one of those meets that the head track coach of a Buffalo College approached me. He said that he had been to a number of meets, and he observed my performance. He proceeded to tell me that he would like me to run for the college team. This, of course, meant that I would have to be a student. I was astounded at these opportunities and how they occurred. I just did not think I would be going to college because I was not that smart. This is what I thought, and what my Dad thought. Mom always said, "You can be whatever you set your mind to." Now I had to make a choice, and it was very clear that it was my choice. I will become a tool and die maker or go to college. I chose college and running. Over the coming years, automation would take the place of people in the tool and die position.

I had to call the track coach and tell him my decision. When I called, he immediately set up an appointment in his office, about two days later. It all seemed to move so fast, and it seemed to be in someone else's control. The day of our appointment came, and as I entered the coach's office, fear set in. I realized how big the school was, and then, I reminded myself that this was a very good man. Then he said, "We are glad to have you on board." He then presented me with my very first training work out. I got up out of the chair, and I was very excited about what had happened and what was next in my life. I turned and walked toward the door to leave. I thanked the coach again, opened the door, and made a step out the door. Suddenly, I realized that I had to have a major. I turned to the coach as I stood in the door and said, "Coach! What am I going to take?" His eyes scanned my body from head to toe and then back up to my head. He leaned back and said,

"You look like an industrial arts/technology teacher." I said, "That sounds good." He then gave me instructions on who to see and what building their office was in. My head was whirling, and I no longer had time to think of fear. I graduated from that college and was the first of the Malinowski family to do so. I eventually was offered a position as teacher and a track coach.

Mr. Ambrose was right! Running would take me somewhere. It's the small decisions that really have the greatest effects on our lives.

LIFE-CHANGING COACH

As a freshman in high school, I walked to the locker room on a sunlit, fall afternoon. The angle of the sun in the fall at four in the afternoon gave a hazy effect to the locker room as the rays of sunlight came through the windows at a very low angle. This reflected the dust particles in the air as they hit the row of lockers on the right wall of the team room. Charley was sitting on the bench in his practice uniform and full pads. I had great respect for Charley, and I asked him how I could join the football team. He explained what he had done to join and whom I should talk to. The next thing I knew, I was in those sweaty, smelly pads getting the snot knocked out of me from every angle. I had to learn more about the game itself, and at times, it all seemed very overwhelming. I had never played organized football before. After about three weeks, I decided I did not need to do this that badly, but I did not tell anyone.

One evening after doing the dinner dishes, Mom and I were in the car on the way to the drug store. This was where model airplanes were sold. I told Mom that I was definitely not enjoying the football practice, and I was thinking about quitting. She very calmly said that that would change if I would just give it three more weeks. In her wisdom, she was right. It did start to be fun even though I was still getting my head handed to me. Sometimes, I had it coming.

I had a classmate in my algebra class who was about six foot tall, and I was five foot eight. He sat on the other side of the room from me. One noticeable quality about him was his very red hair. I would wait until the teacher was about to enter the room and then yell out, "Hey, Red Rodent." The second day I did it, he figured out who was yelling at him, as I grinned and looked back at his angry, red face. He just silently mouthed, "I will get you." I think I must have been doing this for the thrill of his hunt. After class, he came blasting out of that room into the hallway. The chase was on. It was all very exciting because I knew I could outrun him. This went on for a week and two days. I would scream "Red Rodent" in the hallway, and his head would turn so fast I thought it would come off of his neck. He would see me and take off in pursuit while I would be laughing away at his efforts.

Then it happened. I was on the junior varsity team, and the coach announced that we were scrimmaging the varsity that afternoon. This was a sometimes occurrence and not out of the ordinary. We lined up for the first play, and the play went away from me, so I was just standing there. Then suddenly, it seemed as though the entire world had decided to hit me and knock me to the ground. I laid there, face up, with a monster breathing through his facemask and looking straight into my helmet. I was so stunned by this painful hit that it took a second to figure out what had happened. Then this beast just said, "Red Rodent huh!"

I only weighed about a hundred and forty pounds. The coach had me at a right guard position. I was a stringy, scared boy most of the time—but I learned the game. I now knew that if I could survive the blind side hit of Red Rodent, I could take most of any hits. Football would now become fun.

At the beginning of my sophomore season, the assistant JV coach saw that I could catch the football. He told me that I was now an end. As the season came to a close, I was running plays from the fullback position. That was the position I played throughout my junior year.

I watched the University of Buffalo football replays of games on TV. I had noticed a player named Maue, and he was very good. He played running back and was an outstanding defensive back. This was quite an accomplishment because UB was the best team in the northeast at that time. I told Mom—after watching one of the UB game replays—that I wanted to be a starting running back. She just said, "Be patient, your time is coming." It was always "be patient and it will come to you."

Later that summer, I received a letter from school—stating that we had a new head coach. The wind of change was in motion because Coach Maue signed the letter. I remember reading that letter over and over at least fifty times that week. It was like a rebirth for our team and myself. To top it off, he was a person I already greatly admired for his performance on the field and was an inspiration just by his signature. What was he like as a person? We all would find out in a matter of three weeks. We were about to be transformed by his willpower.

I admired coach Maue from day one. His first talk at our first practice was about winning. He explained that we would only have about eight plays to the right and the same to the left side of the line. We all looked at each other as he continued to say that we would not need a playbook because we were going to practice those plays until we could walk in our sleep through them. This was going to be work. Coach Maue said that once we had these plays perfected, we would have the time of our life playing football. This was a very different concept from having a playbook with about eighty plays in it, and you were to memorize them all.

I remember someone asking could we win with only eight plays. This was the conversation in the locker room. I quietly thought to myself, I believe him. This is Coach Maue—a member of a Lambert Trophy college team. It was not easy to take a losing attitude and make it a winning attitude, but the process was under way.

Coach Maue was about five feet ten inches tall, and his assistant coach was about five feet eight. Both men were in very good shape. They could terrorize us at will because we were starting to submit to their ways. When I say terrorize, I mean in a very positive way. We greatly admired both Coach Maue and Coach Backus, who was the line coach. They were both in their mid-twenties, but to us, they were examples of real men. They both exuded honesty, integrity and very high morals, but they also loved the idea of full contact at full speed. Every lineman was bigger, physically, than Coach Backus, and yet, he could knock any of them on their butt, and they all knew it. We all knew that these men knew about commitment. They showed us through their actions how committed they were. You never mess with a committed person unless you are more committed.

Both coaches never talked down to us but always looked deep into our eyes. That was scary at first, and then, you knew the coach just wanted your total attention because he was giving you his. We were approached as winners from the day we received Coach Maue's letter from the previous summer.

On some practices, the frustration became apparent. Coach Maue would grab the facemask of your helmet and yell, "Look at me and listen." He would give only three- to five-word instructions. He wanted us to focus on the task and the game itself. He would always repeat that once you could do that, you would have fun playing the game. He always gave you a punch on the shoulder pads after his verbal blasting. At first, we thought he was mad, but soon we learned that he was very focused. Champions are always that way. He was the first thoroughbred champion, outside of Dad, who was put into my life.

It was the first week of September, and we were practicing a play called "the 26." It was a sweep with the fullback carrying the ball to the outside of the end. The tailbacks' job was to run downfield ahead of the fullback and find someone to block. I was the tailback, and I missed the block. Coach Maue just shook his head and called me over to him. He looked at me as he said he could not believe I would run all that way, do all that work, and not complete the last part of the play. I needed to find someone and hit him with a block. That thought process enlightened me right there on the spot. I remembered that twenty-second lecture because it applies to all that we do in life. You can do all kinds of work to get to a certain point and then not complete the very last task. No matter how minor the task was, you come up short. We ran the play again, and I completed my assignment. I thought it was a profound event back then, and I still do to this very day.

We went to our first game and got beaten by the eventual league champion East Aurora by a score of 31 to 13. We actually started to play Coach's game in the fourth quarter. I came out of the game with about six minutes remaining. I was standing a little bit behind Coach Maue for about two plays when he exploded with what happened on the field. He turned around, and there I was. He stated he had had enough of this crap, and at the same time, in a flash, he was reaching out with his right hand. As he went to grab the front part of my shoulder pads, below my neck, he raked his fingernails down the front of my neck. When his fingers reached the shoulder pads, he gripped on very tightly and yanked me over to his face. He looked me straight in the eyes and yelled, "I want you to go in there and run a 28 sweep and score a touchdown now!" He then threw me toward the huddle at the center of the field. When my feet hit the ground, I continued to run to the huddle and told Billy, our quarterback, "Coach wants a 28 sweep." That meant I carried the ball around the right end. I did what Coach had said, and we scored our first touchdown. What came to my mind much later was that he had commanded it. We executed the play as he said, and it happened. I believed at that point we started to realize that we could be winners. The last six minutes of that game were actually fun—just as he said it would be. We won the next four games.

Coach Maue and Backus were starting to have fun too. One practice, they both came out in full pads and played pass defense against the backs and the receivers. We started laughing until the first pattern was run. The receiver was smacked to the ground, and the pass was intercepted. We all got real serious—fast. They would hit us and yell, "Get up." Sometimes they would take the ball right out of our hands. These guys were not only tough, they were good. Coach Backus just amazed us with his running and leaping for such a little man. When we were done with practice, they were laughing at us and with us. We knew we had real men coaching us, who loved us without saying so. Those two wanted to win in all that they did.

After practice, we were all talking when we were in the shower. We were comparing how they would blast us to the ground with a clean hit and then yell, "Get up and beat me next time." When you did beat them they would slap you on the helmet and yell, "Good job, that's how to do it, now do it on game day." We always hoped they would do it again but they did not need to.

After every Saturday game, we had a dance in the evening. We never had any night games because lights cost too much. At one dance, both of our football coaches were the chaperones. For some of us on the team, this was really extra special. Then we found out that Coach Maue was bringing a date with him. She was a very attractive blond lady. Coach was very busy chaperoning when he walked over to me and asked me to dance with his date. He wanted me to take care of her because he was very busy, and she was just standing around. He told me to treat her like a lady and proceeded to walk away. He must have noticed how nervous I had become because he stopped in his tracks, turned around, looked me in the eye and said, "Ted, just be the person that you are." I was so honored by his words and by his trust. That trust brings tears to my eyes as I am writing this. He has influenced my life in so many ways. I must say that he is a true hero in my life. He is a very humble man with an enormous heart. His trust and his life-building sayings have profoundly affected my life. I think of him often, and I am very grateful that he was placed in my life by Providence.

Coach made a statement about our team about twenty-five years later when I saw him. He said that some teams he had coached had far more talent than our team, but our team had an awesome desire to win more than any other team he had coached. That was enough for me.

All of this because Mom said to stick it out for three more weeks, and your time is coming.

Finding "The One"

The basketball games on Friday night were always fun to go to. If the team won, they were even more fun. Tom, Dave, Ron, and I would always sit together, yell and talk, and have a good time being friends. The game would be over at about eight thirty in the evening, and for fifty cents, one could go to the dance in the auxiliary gym. These dances were stand against the wall and watch affairs. Once in a while, one of us would actually get enough nerve to ask a girl to dance. I don't think any of us realized that all those girls were just waiting for anyone of us to ask them to dance. It was better that none of the guys knew that. To us, it was almost like making a commitment just dancing with a girl. Of course, that was not how any of the girls saw it.

One Friday, I purchased a six-inch-diameter sucker and proceeded to the water fountain where I soaked it with water a number of times until it became very sticky. As I entered the dance, I saw my friend Lance had already asked someone to dance. I very calmly walked over to Lance and slapped him on the cheek with that very sticky sucker. I thought for sure that when Lance put his cheek against his partner's, they would stick together. This was not a pleasant experience for him, and he let me know it. This dance stuff was now becoming a very serious ritual to some of the participants. I did not know that my time was coming for such an experience.

My time came in my senior year. It was a March of Dimes dance. This one was seventy-five cents for an important cause. I saw her there, and I slowly walked toward her. As I stood in front of her, I asked her to dance, and she softly said, "Yes." Our first dance was a fast dance—so we were apart, and I saw her beautiful, long-flowing, brown hair. I was taken by to the vision of God's very own creation. She smiled, and I was crazed in what seemed to be the most perfect smile I had ever seen. This different feeling was upon me, and I was completely infatuated in this vision. Nothing else existed but what I saw in front of me. She was wearing a pink, fluffy woven sweater with a V-neck. She wore a gold, heart-shaped necklace. Her pleated skirt had a plaid pattern of blues and grays with a pink thread going through the plaid pattern. Her shoes were black flats with webbing over her toes, and she had gorgeous legs. She had my attention.

The next dance was a slow dance, and I asked her again. My heart jumped with her positive answer. Then, it was announced that this was the last dance of the night. I had a feeling deep in my heart that this girl would be very special for the rest of my life. This feeling was shouting to me. I wondered what feeling she had. As we parted, I knew our lives were just starting to flow together. I watched from a distance as she walked off the dance floor, and as she walked out into the cold night wind, I saw her beautiful, brown hair move around her shoulders as she disappeared into her father's car. I knew we were destined to be together, but did she?

It is really unique that when our emotions for someone increase, every song seems to be for you and your situation. It was as if The Beach Boys, The Lettermen, and a new group called The Beatles were watching our lives and singing just for our hearts. I was astounded to find out that the girl I had danced with lived a half mile from my home.

The following Monday I saw her at school, and I had to ask her to the next dance. She accepted. Wow!

Everytime I saw her, my whole being seemed to jump with a kind of calm excitement. The mystery is how and why this kind of thing happens. I did not ask that question then because I was lovesick on whatever the body produces to give you that wonderful feeling. It always starts so small and simple. I would look for her in the main school hallway as I walked with the guys on our normal morning patrol before homeroom. There she was! Focus is a very powerful thing. It was focus that caused me to completely ignore my patrol buddies and walk toward her. Nothing else existed at that very moment but the vision of her. There were many sounds at the student lockers. The morning talks about every event, or the books falling from a locker shelf with a very loud whack did not distract me. It was like a gun going off but I never heard it.

What I could hear was the soft swishing sound of her skirt. It was like the warm summer breezes gently swishing the tall field grass back and forth. I knew I could hear her hair moving with that same sound, just a little softer as she walked. When she smiled as I approached, I could hear her lips move across her teeth, and also, the very quiet opening and closing of those big brown eyes. All she said was "Hi!" That was all it took to make the entire day. Oh! It was wonderful to be in high school. This whole experience became a daily habit that I did not want to kick.

My buddies just shook their heads because they were very quickly being replaced. Eventually, each one of them would find their own experience. Only one of my buddies really had the same experience with his girl that I had. He just said, "Wow!" I looked at him, and he knew that I knew exactly what he meant.

In the cold days of that winter, we would take walks from our own homes and meet at the corner in between them and then walk together. We always would meet under the same streetlight. Sometimes, the snow would be falling ever so slowly and gently. As I approached her, I could see her waiting in that light. Darkness was everywhere but where she was standing. The perfect white snow falling from the heavens and into the dark and then into the bright white light that encircled her. It was as if she was standing in a ball covered with glass. She put out her glove-covered hand and just said "Hi!" I took her hand and said "Hi" as we walked out of the light and into the darkness together. The snow seemed to be like angel dust—protecting both of us. Suddenly, it was not cold, but we could still see our breath. As we walked, we passed by a stand of pine trees, which were about twenty feet tall. The stand had to stretch for a good forth of a mile. Their branches sagging with the weight of the pure white snow was peaceful. A very slight gust of wind came up and swirled some of the fine powder up off of the pines as we walked by. Gently, the loving hand of the wind moved her hair next to and across my face. It seemed to wave her perfume to me. The air was so fresh and chilled that the scent seemed to be even stronger than normal. The warmth inside me caused the chill to leave. We just stopped walking and wrapped our arms around one another. The warmth of caring for each other is the great heater of life. There was no passionate attacking of each other, but rather, a very gentle embrace in the middle of what seemed like falling crystals. Any other type of embrace would have caused the crystal flakes to shatter, and the pine tree branches to break. They were the only witnesses to a developing deep love.

There has never been another.

THE GIFTS FROM OTHERS

D ad worked for a distribution company which was owned by a
family who were very generous to my father. Dad could have
worked for a car manufacturer but turned it down out of loyalty. Although he worked very long hours, he would sometimes
bring home very unexpected surprises. One Friday in January,
he brought home a six-wheeled vehicle which could carry two
people and some cargo behind the bench seat. The body was dark
red in color with three big and fat balloon-type tires on each
side. It certainly looked very strange sitting on that trailer behind
Dad's station wagon. It was 1966, and these kinds of toys were
extremely expensive and very rare. I couldn't imagine what a person would do with such a contraption. Dad knew exactly what
we would be doing for the next month with this remarkable toy.
We were far from monetary wealth, but we knew those who had
wealth and were very generous with it.

Dad got into the machine, and he looked like he was going
to burst into a long and loud "Yahoo!" That was not how he was.
Dad just smiled and gave an extremely approving nod of his head.
The red color of the machine against the beautiful, white, clean
and crunchy snow was really an awesome sight.

The one-inch flakes of snow were beginning to fall, and every
once in a while, the sun would burst forth giving the effect of
an old-time photoflash going off. This would cause rainbows to

flash on those big snowflakes. It did nothing to their taste as they struck our tongues.

Dad broke the silence of the moment when he said, "Get in." He turned the key to the left on that red dashboard where a red light showed you the machine was on. The only other feature was a speedometer. There was one small and straight black plastic seat with a formed backrest that was cold and hard but would soon be known as a "back saver." The two-cycle engine burst into life, and the smell of the oil and gasoline was like perfume to a young boy's nostrils. Dad pulled back on the two sticks which controlled each side of the machine, separately. By pulling back on both sticks, both sides backed up with the same amount of power. Dad, ever so slowly, backed the machine off of the trailer and drove it on the flat, snow-covered ground. He immediately took me on a trip to the summer fair with the ride that followed. Wow!

The rest of the month was a race to get home: fire up that beast and roar out of the yard in a plume of blue smoke with flying, powdered snow on the six-wheeled adventure. You just didn't know what was in store when you were blasting through the empty fields. In the early evening, my brother John and I were blasting through a field. We were sitting still when a dog came out after us. I started the machine and took off. The dog began to fall behind us but was persistently running after our white cloud of snow. I pulled back on one stick and pushed the other one full forward. The result was a perfect, one hundred eighty degree turn at wide-open throttle. We were turning and sliding on the snow in one direction, and when the machine came around to where it was pointing in the opposite direction, I pushed both sticks completely forward. We were now sliding backward until the tires got traction on the snow. The dog stopped running and in fact, put his front paws out in front of him to stop. He seemed to come to attention and stare in disbelief because we were now chasing him faster and faster. It was as if he did a double take because it was something he had never seen before. The dog took off running. We were about fifteen yards behind him. As he was running, he kept turning to see if we were still coming. The dog turned, and we turned with the same abruptness. He then headed for a ditch which was about four feet deep, with some water in it. He jumped the stream and then stopped and turned. I stopped the machine at the edge of the ditch. It was now dusk so I turned on the headlights. The lights shined on the dog's feet as he stood on a berm about four feet high on the other side of the ditch. I jammed both sticks forward and hit the gas. The machine lurched forward and went through the ditch and began to climb the berm. The headlights were now pointing up on the dog. It was as if he had a facial expression of utter amazement on his face. He finally regained his senses and took off into the safety of the darkness. This all took place in about four minutes. It seemed like half an hour of fun. I stopped the machine. My brother and I laughed at this creature, which to us, took on human qualities. We never had an experience with a dog and the machine again. They all seemed to stay clear of it.

My sister Becky decided to try her hand at the machine. She was so excited to get her solo shot at driving the red monster. She left on her own and headed for the field that was behind our house. An hour later, she walked into the house crying. She had managed to get three flat tires. We went out to the field to see the red machine sitting on top of an old bedspring someone had used to drag the soil for planting, maybe ten years before. We all laughed because out of forty acres of field, she had to find the bedsprings. She was determined to drive the monster. After the tires were fixed, she took it out again but was rather timid with the machine so as not to break it.

We had many joyful rides that winter all because someone else had great bounty and grace, and they were willing to share it with us. We were all very grateful.

Dad under Fire

Dad made sure that I was always learning the importance of work and that money just did not grow on trees. He said that when I was sixteen, we would work together. True to his words, in the summer of my sixteenth year, we began by washing the beer trucks used by the distribution company he worked for.

Every Saturday morning, except for football season, we would go to a small restaurant and have a hard roll and a cup of coffee for breakfast. We then would read the sports section of the newspaper. It really was a very important time with Dad sitting at the counter of various coffee shops discussing what the pro football teams would be doing and sometimes, even topics about life. That was a real rarity with Dad. He would ask if I was ready to go, and we would leave for the "shop" as he called it. Once we got there, we would each grab a bucket with wheels on it and a brush, along with a handful of soap powder which we threw into the bucket before we filled it with water. We each had a hose to soak down each truck before we washed it with the soapy brush. Then, we would reach to the top of those trucks rinsing off the soap. There were about thirty trucks, and about twenty of them were inside. The few that were outside could be washed outside in the summer and rotated inside in the winter. Dad had it down to a system, and it worked very well.

One Saturday in late June, we were on our way to wash trucks at about seven thirty in the morning. Dad decided to stop at a restaurant in a local plaza about eight miles from our house. On the way, Dad would have a cigarette. He would always crack his window because he knew I didn't smoke. As he turned into the plaza parking lot, he just said that we were going to this restaurant because they have better coffee. As we drove through the lot, the radio newsman was talking about a drive-by shooting in the city. The windows of some bar had been shot out.

Dad parked the car in the parking space, and the radio went off when Dad turned the car off. We got out of the car and stepped into the brilliant sunlight on that beautiful morning. As we walked to the curb in front of the restaurant, you could see the dark blue water of Lake Erie in the distance, along with Canada and the city of Buffalo skyline. It was as if you could jump from cloud to cloud right on to the white and gold-colored buildings of the city about eight miles across the water. We were on the side of a hill looking down and over the lake. It was a gorgeous sight, and a very joyful morning to be alive and having time with Dad. We entered the restaurant through a glass door after walking past a twenty-foot-long, plate glass window, which was about six feet high across the entire front of the restaurant.

As we walked over to the counter, you could see that it was shaped like the letter M with the indentation in the middle. Dad decided to pick the two seats that were in the center of the indentation so that the counter was curving around beside us on both sides of our seats. We were the only customers in this empty restaurant. As we leaned against the counter in front of us, the waiter came over and poured our coffee. He asked if we wanted any food. We both ordered a fried hard roll. The waiter walked back and gave our order to the cook.

Suddenly, there was a very loud bang. My mind, in a split second, said that it was a gunshot. In the time it took my head to snap from looking at the waiter to looking to the front of the restaurant, Dad had already hit the deck and had his hand on my shoulder pulling me out of that seat as he shouted, "Get down."

We were both on the floor, surrounded by the counter up above, when Dad yelled to cover my head. As we lay on the floor for no more than two seconds, we heard two more very loud bangs. I knew that this had to be the same shooters from the city. After the second bang, the front plate glass window shattered, and all the glass fragments were blown into the restaurant. The shards of glass blew right over the top of the counters on each side of us on their way to the back of the room where you could hear the glass hitting the back wall of the restaurant. There was a combination of the tinkling of glass and the whoosh of the wind, but not a single piece of anything ever struck either one of us. In the next instant, Dad grabbed me by the back of my shirt and pulled me up off the floor. He said, "Let's get out of here now!" He was actually pushing me in the back as we moved faster and faster for the door. The only thing left was the aluminum framework that was supporting the glass. I became very concerned because the guys with the guns could still be out there in their car, but I never verbalized that thought because Dad knew what he was doing.

As we stepped off the curb in front of the restaurant and onto the pavement of the parking lot, I turned to see the restaurant engulfed in flames. We began to run as the flames came out the front like a blowtorch. When we reached the car, we drove away from the flames fast. We both got out of the car and were standing with two of the workers from the restaurant. It was no more than four minutes since Dad had pulled me to the floor. Dad looked around, and quickly he said, "Which one of you is the cook?" One of the workers said, "Neither one of us." Dad then muttered that he was still in there. He then took about three quick steps toward the inferno, and I yelled, "No, you are not going in there!" as I grabbed the back of his shirt. A car broke through the smoke and was coming toward us. It was the cook who had gone out the back of the restaurant to save his car. I was so relieved because I didn't know how I would have held my Dad back from going in for that cook. We never did get our coffee and hard roll.

We got into the car after the police took our names and went to another restaurant for our hard roll and coffee. That was when Dad explained what actually had happened.

There was a paint store next to the restaurant, and some old paint cans mixed with some oily rags caught fire by spontaneous combustion. The loud bangs were the first of the many paint cans that blew up. These explosions blew out the front of the paint store window. When this happened, the air in the store blew out the front also. This resulted in the air in the restaurant being sucked out and over to the paint store. That was why the plate glass window was pulled into the restaurant in a thousand pieces. It caused a partial vacuum in the restaurant. The paint store had all the fuel it needed to be a raging inferno, which only caused more oil-based paint cans to blow and add more fuel, causing the blowtorch effect.

There were no gunmen. My imagination had just run rampant. What Dad did that day was as if he was on automatic pilot. I witnessed him in action in a critical situation, and he made all the right decisions without hesitation. I am sure that his military experience and training, along with a great heart to help, had a giant input on all of this. I had a great respect for the man he was and even more admiration. I feel very blessed that he was my Dad. He said nothing about what happened to anyone, unless they asked. His answer contained no description or detail. It was no brag, just facts. I heard him describe it as an interesting morning. He was the model for the phrase, "Action speak louder than words."

As I think back to some of the things he did, I am listening to him more intently now more than when he was on this earth with me. I know who his teacher is.

BOBBY'S GENEROSITY

Having a friend is a real joy in life. To have a good friend when you are just short of five years old is truly remarkable. Bobby was that for me.

It all started in the summer of my fifth birthday. I would walk down the street which had no sidewalks, and two cars a day might pass by. That did not count our parents. My purpose was to get to Bobby's house to talk and play. It was a glorious day of eighty degrees. The slight breeze transported just a hint of the lake to our houses.

Rita, who was Bobby's mom, brought out Bobby's tricycle that had a chain drive to the rear wheels. The pedals were not on the front wheel as with most tricycles. The pedals were like those on a two-wheeled bike with a chain which drove the gear mounted on the rear axle which was connecting the two back wheels. My normal tricycle was very small compared to this beast. His bike was silver with a sixteen-inch wheel on the front and two twelve-inch wheels on the back. I had a twelve-inch wheel on the front of my tricycle. Rita could see that I was going to have a very hard time keeping up with Bobby's tricycle. Her solution was to bring out a second tricycle, which was much bigger but not as big as Bobby's. It had the normal pedal arrangement, and I could keep up very well. Rita was always a very kind and generous lady. I never called her Rita when addressing her. It was always Mrs. Herdle.

Bobby and I would ride the road between our houses over and over that hot summer. It was a distance of three hundred feet, but it sure seemed to be a long way. Whenever a car would come, we would pull off into the grass on the side of the road and wait for the car to pass. We always made sure that we were both on the same side of the road. Bobby told me that the law said that this was the correct procedure. We always tried to obey the law with our vehicles. We also believed that we would be safe if we obeyed the laws.

People always slowed when they passed in their cars. Some would wave and say, "Hi boys." In our small town, everyone seemed to know each other. Any stranger would really stick out.

When the weather became rainy or cold, we would ride around in the open basement of Bobby's house. We became very attached to those bikes. It also made our hearts and bodies—especially our legs, very strong and durable.

One day, we were riding in the basement and took our break to go upstairs for a treat. It was about three in the afternoon, and Bobby's mom asked if I would like some, as she held out a small bowl with a new treat in it. I answered with a yes. I reached into the bowl and took out one of the delights and placed it into my mouth. The salt rolled off and onto my tongue with just a touch of cooking oil. These were just plain great to taste. The crunch when you bit into them was very satisfying. I wanted more. They were almost addictive. That afternoon, I went home and told my mom about this new food called potato chips. She stated that they were very expensive, but she would check it out.

They were really just new to me, and anything new was very exciting. I could not wait for snack time whenever we were at Bobby's house. We did not always have potato chips, but I would request them.

The seasons passed, and two or three more years passed along with them. We were both now in school. The school year was done, and we were both enjoying the hot summer days again.

We were sitting on the cement steps leading to the front door of Bobby's brick home. Bobby asked if I wanted to play a game, and I said yes. He went into the house and came out with a black and red checkerboard. He laid it down on the cool and refreshing cement of the front porch, which was now in the shade of the afternoon. He told me about this game called checkers as he laid the actual checkers on the board in the appropriate places. I listened as he explained the rules along with his mom, who was sitting in a chair relaxing and observing. We must have played five games. He beat me every time. I was catching on though, because each game took longer. I could see that there was a strategy involved. We played more that summer, and I got to where I could beat him. We even played checkers in the winter.

The following summer, Bobby introduced me to the game of chess. He would beat me all the time, but I now knew that, eventually, I would beat him if I would pay attention and learn. Sometimes, we would just jump up and hit the grass—wrestling to get some activity going between games of chess. Bobby was about three inches taller than me. Soon, it became difficult to beat him. I knew that if I wrestled him enough, I would figure out a way to beat him. It was just a matter of time. He never once tried to actually hurt me. I would surprise him with a move and be on the verge of victory. That was when his size would be to his advantage to get me pinned. He knew I would be persistent and not quit. He was a good friend.

The seasons turned to winter again, and we were all heading into the joyful season of Christmas. The air would finally turn cold, and I knew it conducted the electricity of Christmas much better than warm air. It seemed so charged that you could see the sparks fly. The transformers on the telephone poles hummed their tune in the cold.

It was the first week of December, and Bobby took me to his room. There on the floor, in front of me, was a four by eight sheet of plywood. On it was a Lionel electric train set. It was my first real life experience with the almost mystical electric train. The sounds and motion captivated me completely. I followed Bobby into the room and sat down on the floor next to him. He was sitting at the transformer. He fired up that train, and when he blew the whistle of the steamer, my heart seemed to leap. We turned off the lights of the room and closed the door and pulled the window shades down. The sight was almost overwhelming to a young boy.

Bobby ran the train and showed me how to operate the switching track sections. I wanted to run the train. I wanted the throttle. He knew it because he did let me run the train itself for about ten minutes. That was enough to settle down the passion for a little while.

Every Christmas, he would receive a new piece of equipment. One year, he received a switcher—which meant that he now had two engines. I thought that I could run one, and he could run the other. Because of electrical technicalities, that was not possible.

Mom knew how excited I was for a train, and that Christmas, I received a Marx steamer set. It was very exciting, and I was thankful. But it was not a Lionel. It was an electric train, and I was still very happy. This gift was good for years. I actually wore it out. I always looked forward to Christmas and time at Bobby's house.

One year, Bobby received a chemistry set. He was extremely excited because he actually loved chemistry and science. I would just sit next to him in the basement where the set was set up on a table against the cement wall. I enjoyed watching him perform simple experiments. He really enjoyed doing them. He would always explain what he was going to do and the procedure as he did it. Sometimes, I would even understand what he was doing.

The seasons changed from winter to spring, and we loved the cycle of seasons. We were still doing chemistry.

We had both been watching *The Adventures of Wild Bill Hickock* and *The Roy Rogers Show* on the TV. They were on every Saturday morning. Many of the shows involved a shipment of nitroglycerin going somewhere. The bad guys were always trying to steal the wagons shipping the stuff. Bobby thought he could make nitro with his chemistry set. This sounded very exciting and scary at the same time.

One really sunny, warm April day, I watched as he explained the combination of certain substances which were in the set. He was combining them as I watched. The liquid results were in a test tube. Bobby had placed the test tube in a rack on the table in front of us. We both just stared at his creation for a few minutes. Finally, Bobby broke the silence. He said, "If the substance starts to boil, we are in trouble." That meant we had the real thing, and it could blow. We both continued to stare at the amber-colored substance in that test tube. Suddenly, fear increased to terror as we saw the bubbles start to rise in the liquid. My eyes must have grown in size. Bobby noticed that I was tongue-tied as I tried to get his attention. I could not get out the words: "It is boiling." He glanced at the test tube and just said, "Wow." I was astounded to see Bobby checking his formulas and procedures which he had written down. Then, he looked at me and said that we must get this test tube outside and dilute the amber liquid with lots of water. He gently lifted the test tube out of the rack. He then pro-ceeded to walk slowly to the stairs leading out of the basement. I was right behind him. When he reached the top of the stairs, I reached around him and opened the backdoor of the house. When he stepped over the door threshold to the outside, I felt an incredible release of tension. I guess it was because I knew the house was now safe. As Bobby walked carefully down the three steps to the backyard, I went straight for the hose that was coiled up right next to the step. I turned on the hose while I was uncoil-ing it. Bobby began to pour out the liquid on the shale-covered ground. He told me to run the water all over that area. I was even afraid to walk on that spot. I was afraid it could still blow. He looked at me and said. "I think we really made it, but we will never do that again."

We never really knew if we made nitroglycerin. We both took a deep breath and decided this was way too much excitement.

As the years went on into high school, we remained friends. Bobby grew to be six foot two inches tall and over two hundred pounds. He made a good offensive tackle on the varsity football team, and I was a running back. He blocked for me on many running plays. He was one of those gentle big men with a great heart. He also became a chemist. He introduced me to many new games and pleasures and actually helped arouse my curiosity about anything new.

You just never know why certain people have been placed into your life. I know now why he was put into my life. He was a great example of a person who was smart, generous, honest, and showed great integrity. Exactly the kind of friend a very young boy should have. I did not pick him, but I know who did.

Hey You

Every boy should have a dog. That is what a boy of eight thinks. Dad and Mom must have been thinking the very same thing, because one day, Dad came home with a very noisy box. He walked through the front door carrying the noisy, cardboard box and a great, big grin. He never spoke a word and neither did Mom. They both knew what was in the box, and Dad and Mom were both in agreement. This all was happening after Dad came home from work, and it was a fall day, so the angle of the sun coming in that front door was beginning to grow dim. This made it hard to see what was in the box, but whatever it was, it must have been very big and scary. It was clawing on the sides of the box and snarling to get out.

My sister Anne and I were a little afraid to open the box and look in. We did not want to let this monster loose in our house. We both kept looking at Mom and Dad for advice. They just stood there—grinning and never said a word. I finally managed to grab one of the flaps on the top of the box while Anne grabbed the other flap like a bolt of lightning. We both gave a quick pull, and the monster inside saw the opening and took it. We both drew back our hands in surprise. The monster made a very quick decision to leap out of the box. We both started laughing as the blur of black and white fur attacked our faces with its wet tongue and beat us with its waging tail of joy. The monster was a puppy, which was so glad to have a home and a family that would love him.

We had no idea what to name him but that did not matter now. We had our very own dog. He was only about three months old, and we knew he just wanted to be with us. I think he was a cross between a Beagle and a Dalmatian. Dad and Mom just said he was a mongrel. We thought he was just like us.

The few warm days of fall would be good days to take the puppy outside in the front yard of our house and play. He would run and jump, as we would call out, "Hey You, come here." Eventually, that was all he would respond to. We had named our dog, and whenever we called him, we got everyone's attention.

Hey You loved Dad. When Dad would come home from work, he would sit down in his overstuffed recliner and read the newspaper. Little Hey You would jump up into Dad's lap and lick his face, and Dad would be belly laughing while he was trying to say "Stop!" He could never get that word out because of all the laughing by him and us. I think it was the laughter of love that caused that dog to settle down and lay down right on Dad's lap as he read the newspaper. Soon, you could hear Dad start to snore, and the newspaper would start its slow decent to Dad's lap from the reading position. Under that newspaper, you could hear the snoring of little Hey You. It was wonderful thing to hear and see. Hey You gave Dad great joy, and he made us all wag our tails.

As the winter snow began to fall outside, Mom made sure that Hey You did his dirty work in a cardboard box. One Saturday, Dad was home, and he got a whiff of the dog box. After that, he said dogs go outside. He picked up Hey You just as he was saying those words, and he threw him out the front door and into a snowdrift in our front yard. Anne and I were speechless because we thought he was gone. As we stood looking at the snowdrift, suddenly, Hey You poked his head up through the snowdrift. He seemed to look around as though he was getting his bearings.

Once he spotted where the front door of our house was, he came running like a lightning bolt for the front door of our house. He actually put his head down in the snow and bore a tunnel right to the source of all the cheering being done by his family. Our fears turned into laughter, as we all yelled for Dad to throw him in the snow again. Dad never said a word as Hey You jumped up into his hands. He then proceeded to throw Hey You out farther into the snow with the same result. Two times were enough, so Dad lifted Hey You up and gave him a hug and brought him back into our warm home. Hey You did his dirty work outside from then on. He was now housebroke.

Dad was working two jobs, so he was not always home at dinnertime. Sometimes, he got home after we all went to bed. As Hey You grew bigger, we were not up to see him greet Dad when he got home. One night, Dad was home for supper with us. He sat down in his favorite chair and lifted the paper to read it. Suddenly, Hey You jumped up and smashed into Dad's paper as he was trying to jump into Dad's lap. Dad was laughing with a great belly laugh as all of us of joined him. Hey You stayed up on Dad's lap and just kept circling his lap and licking Dad's face with his tongue while waging and hitting Dad in the face with his waging tail as he turned round and round. Hey You seemed to be almost gleeful as he smashed the paper down. Dad was laughing and trying to keep Hey You's tail and tongue out of his own mouth and eyes. All this while he was laughing so hard, and he was crying, and we were rolling on the floor with laughter. Mom came into the room to see what the noise was all about. The sight she saw had to be just eye-opening. I was on the floor laughing while Anne was leaning against the couch laughing. Dad was sitting in his chair with his hair all messed up from Hey You's tail wagging. Streams of laughter and tears were running down Dad's face. Hey You was standing on a totally destroyed newspaper on Dad's lap. He jumped up on all fours and stood at attention when

Mom entered the room. His tail wagged briskly in Dad's face. Mom immediately joined in our laughter. Then she looked at Hey You and told him to get down.

We all had now witnessed the growth of our dog.

One day that spring, Dad called us all into the living room and explained that we would have to give Hey You away. My sister and I were very upset. The reason was that our neighbor Mrs. Dean thought that Hey You had gotten into their chicken coup and killed a chicken. I thought it was a fox, but it did not matter. We either gave the dog away, or she would have it shot.

Dad took the dog in the car the next day. He had managed to do this without any of us even seeing him do it. When he returned, he called us together with Mom. He told us he had taken Hey You to the SPCA, and when he was there, a very wealthy man came in and took Hey You to his new home. The man owned lots of land, and Hey You would be very happy with lots of room to run free.

Dad said that Hey You gave us great joy, and we needed to be happy for him now. We never had another dog like him!

PAPER ROUTE TO TRAIN ROUTE

There is always a financial need, and it does not matter if the person is twelve or fifty. Dad always said that money is what makes the world go around. You either have it, or you know someone who has it. Being in the first group is always the best. We were in the second group.

My friend Mike had a paper route. He told me that he was giving it up. Then he asked me if I wanted to take over his route. I just figured that there was some money to be made. The key words are "some money." I told him that I would like to, but I had to talk to my mom and dad first. Then, I would let him know. My brain immediately kicked into overdrive with the excitement of making some money on my own.

Dad and Mom had set the example. Dad worked for a beer distribution company during the day and a soda pop company in the evening. He had two full-time jobs. During the time between Thanksgiving and Christmas, Mom worked for the post office. They set the example of how to work. I didn't only see it in action, I knew it. They did what had to be done for the needs of their family. This was what led me to cut lawns, shovel driveways, and even dig graves for the money.

When I told Mom about the paper route, she reminded me that people desired, needed, and depended upon their evening paper. It was their main source of information—and even enjoyment. People were counting on getting their paper no matter what. I answered that I understood. I knew she meant that I had to be extremely dependable. What I really understood was that I could buy a nice, new bike, a fishing rod and reel, and a Lionel electric train. I actually had a goal and a lot of dreams—and that's what was driving me.

I contacted the supervising paper lady. She distributed the papers to all the delivery boys. I told her that I was ready to go. She said, "Great." I was already counting the profits and not the costs. The paper lady explained that I really was in my own business, and that I had to learn to keep records and show costs of doing business, and especially, do what she called the profit and loss statement. I learned that I would pay her for the papers she put in my box each week no matter what. Once the papers were out of her hands and in mine, they were my property. I learned to count them every day and make sure they were not damaged when I received them. I had to pay attention.

I learned a lesson on my first day of business that summer. I had to leave the ball game I was playing with my friends. It was about three in the afternoon, and I had to start my deliveries. Mom's statement on what the paper meant to people rang in my brain. It became harder as the week went on. Saturday was my collection day. That is when people pay you for the week's deliveries of papers. Some of the people didn't pay on time. This ate into my profits. I started to concentrate on that issue, and I became very disappointed. Mom said that you couldn't allow yourself to do that. She reminded me of why I started this business. She said to give it time, and things will work out—but you have to keep working it. I started the route with seventy-eight customers. My profits should have been about eight dollars a week. That first week's profit was about three dollars. The profits tended to even out over a four-week period.

As the weather grew colder and the snow began to fall, the delivery time became longer. In the summer, it would take about two hours. In the winter, it could take as long as four hours.

Every day was a new adventure on the same route. I always started at my house and turned left out of my driveway. I would go right around the block, or about one square mile. The adventure was all that happened in between when I left and when I returned. It could involve dogs, cats, small children, or just people.

One day, I was reaching the end of my deliveries, and I had one paper left. The people had not paid in two weeks so I needed to collect from them also. The weather was snowy, and ice had formed a coating on the roads and pathways. There were no paved sidewalks on my route. I turned my bike to the left, went off the road, and on to an ice-covered pathway. The ice had taken the shape of a gutter which was about three feet wide and about a hundred fifty feet long. The gutter was gently sloping downward. When I had made my turn, I was not aware of the path being ice-covered, so my speed was a little too high. Because I was going downward, I was actually accelerating. I knew that I was on the edge of control. On my left was a row of ten big and old maple trees. Each one was about two feet in diameter. They were very solid. On my right was a six-foot-high hedgerow of pricker bushes. I had only one paper left in my bag which was draped over the back fender of my bike like a saddlebag. The snow was now causing a visibility problem, and the paper was getting wet. I also was flying down this path too fast despite the condition. My brakes were not working on the ice-covered path. The trees were one foot from the handlebars on my left, and the pricker bushes were one foot from my right hand. I was really blasting down an ice-lined half-pipe. It was extremely exciting. That was when something burst out from the hedge on my right. It hit my right hand so hard that one of its teeth sank into my glove-covered hand. The impact forced me to swerve to the left and up the left side of the half-pipe. I just missed a tree. The creature slid on the ice and went right under my back tire. When I ran over him, it lifted the bike a foot into the air, and at the same time, threw the wet paper into the spokes of my bike. When I came down, I was on the left side of the path sliding to the right side. It was at that moment I saw the creature bounce up off of the ice and ran away—screaming. Since I was looking back, I also could see that the spokes of my bike had shred about three inches of the corner of my last paper. As I was regaining control of my bike, I realized that the creature I had run over was a seven or an eight-year-old-boy. He disappeared from sight just as I got my bike stopped.

I decided to continue on to my last house—which was about seventy feet down the icy path. I carefully stopped and got off of my bike. I grabbed the paper from the bag and ran up to the house. I knocked on the door, and the lady came to the door. I said, "Collecting!" This was the standard paperboy procedure in our area. She went to get her money and paid me. As I handed her the damaged paper, I heard a scream go by my head and run into the house. The boy turned toward me revealing a cut lip. I said I was sorry and started to explain, but the mother said that the boy was a brat and waved for me to go. I gladly left and relived the whole episode in my mind as I slowly rode home through the snowfall.

It was dark now but the clean, white snow actually lit up the ride home. I explained what had happened to Dad and Mom. Dad laughed and wanted to know if she tipped me. Later, I found out that the boy had been waiting for me in the bushes. He was going to hit me in the head with a snowball. I was moving so fast that it threw him all off when he jumped out to do his deed. Life sure is an adventure.

The only thing that kept me working the route was the rewards. One of the rewards was to buy a new bike in the coming summer. Right now, I could only think about the snowfall and the coming of Christmas. All that made me do was to think and dream about Lionel electric trains. My friend Bobby had given me the, the desire for trains, many years before. He had a complete layout with two switches, a switcher engine, and the remote control track section. Boys could play with these toys for hours. Snow and electric trains just seemed to be a pair.

Dad and Mom gave me a steamer by Marx on my eighth Christmas. I ran that train right into the tile of our home. It could have worn a groove in the floor, it seemed. Four years of constant running took its toll on that electric motor.

I was now twelve and having a relaxing time with Mom on a snowy Saturday evening. She noticed a used Lionel steam engine set that was for sale in the want ads. She noticed that the price was what I had in my savings cup. She said she would drive me over to Angola to look at the set the next day. Mom called the number listed in the ad and set up the appointment. I had great difficulty sleeping that night. One of my first dreams was about to come true as a result of working the paper route. Dad just said that the owner should set it up for me so that I could make sure that everything worked before I put down my money. We arrived at the seller's house, and they opened the front door and invited us in. And there, the train set was laid out in a simple oval on the floor. It had two switches, a crane car, a dumping coal car, and a barrel car. The engine was smoking as it ran along the track. The smell of that train smoke was like an expensive perfume that short-circuited my brain. I was in love so much that I just blurted out, "I'll take it." Thank goodness the train was running because the noise kept them from hearing what I said. I just lost all bargaining power when the train smoke took control of my emotions. We made an offer below their asking price, and they took it. I breathed a sigh of relief. We all began to box up all of the train parts, and I gently carried it out to the car. There were two boxes, and the first was very heavy with the engine and transformer. The second had the track and switches. Mom said that my pocket certainly must have been lighter after that purchase. The weight of the boxes made me forget about my pockets being empty. Mom could tell I was extremely excited, and Dad could tell too because

I sat on the black tile floor for the next two days playing with that train. It did not matter that the track came apart because of the constant running, or the derailments—which could be caused by a sister who wanted some attention. I knew there must be a giant layout in heaven because this little one down here gave so much joy. Anne and Becky must have wanted to throw the set out the window because I was constantly telling them not to touch anything. I did teach them how to throw the switches and dump the coal but they could not drive the train—they knew how they could get my attention.

As the winter turned to spring, our activities moved back outdoors, and the train was put away. I continued with my paper route and expanded it to ninety-one customers. I kept putting the profits in the cup. The cup was now filled and overflowing. Dad said that he would buy a four by eight sheet of plywood in the fall for the train. He also said that I could set it up in the back room which was about ten by twelve foot. That was where Mom had her washer and dryer. I set the board up on wooden horses. I had visions of a magnificent layout. It would be set up for the winter and taken down in the spring.

That fall, I bought a used Lionel Wabash diesel engine. I also bought a couple more cars. I purchased a roll of layout grass. Construction would commence upon the first snowfall.

I was already arranging the route the trains would take on my new board. This was all being done in my mind—of course. When we are thinking along a positive line of what can happen, all things seem to look better.

The dogs could bark and bite on the paper route. The weather could be very bad, but I kept thinking of the different ways to layout the track on the train board. The word "layout" was very exciting to say. I knew only rich people had train layouts. We definitely were not rich but we were greatly blessed.

The snow finally began to fall, and I set the layout up. I would deliver my papers, do my homework, and work on the train. Dad and Mom knew exactly where I was. I was learning the importance of planning and electricity. I was also learning about failure and success, over and over. When something worked out, I would call all to watch. Sometimes Anne and Becky would sneak in and take something, or move something. They would be in the kitchen with the door open to my train room. They were watching and waiting to see how long it would take me to notice. The giggling was the giveaway to their stunts. Eventually, Anne got her way and drove the train as did Becky.

When Dad and Mom had people over, they would bring them back to see the trains. They ran so much that I would actually have to stop them to cool them down.

Running in the darkness of the night was so great. I could look across the layout at all the lights and see the snow falling outside as a backdrop. It truly became a portrait in my mind.

Dad and Mom always knew where I was every night—and even better, I knew where they and my sisters were. It was the love. I felt it every time I would leave the coolness of that back room and walk through the door and into the warmth of that little house and great family.

I built a layout with my son, and I am building another one with my grandchildren. The train route had run through my entire life, I was encouraged by my parents and now, my wife. She knows right where I am!!

Two Weeks of the Fourth of July

I have learned that every season has its own beauty. July meant that we were in the very heart of summer, as far as I was concerned. The warmth of the sun and the green of the trees brought on the announcements by the bugs and frogs that summer was near. They all had their unique sounds. Yard care in the summer made you aware of all of these creatures and their sounds. Dad took care of Mr. Bailey's yard when he was growing up and that led to more than yard care as Dad had his own family.

Mr. Bailey owned some property on Chautauqua Lake. Dad rented out the house which was right on the water. He owned more than one house. Dad was able to rent this house on the water for the week before the 4th of July and the week after. We were at the lake for about seven summers in a row. I loved our time there. At that time, it seemed to be about as close to perfection as I would see—short of heaven itself. Each summer that we went there was better than the last. Then again, everything has a season.

This particular season of life started when I was in my eleventh year of life. We would pack the car with clothes and some food and take the drive to Chautauqua Lake. It would be such a long drive of one hour to the lake. It was really only about fifty miles from our home. We drove south into the hills and farms.

The goats and sheep of the area inhabited the hillsides. There were always signs declaring the best goat's milk fudge for sale. Our car never stopped at those signs. Dad would speed the car up a hill and crest it. Anne's, Becky's, and my stomach would tickle like crazy as were dropped down the other side of the hill. We would all be in laughter, and then Dad would already be up on the next hill. We were approaching this long hill, and Mom said that we needed to look out the front of the car and observe all we could. We came to the top of the hill and saw a sign which said "Welcome to Mayville, New York." Our heads turned to look straight ahead again as we entered the village. We were heading down a slight incline into a town teaming with people. They walked along on the sidewalks that had flowerpots hanging from the lampposts. Flowers surrounded the bases of the lampposts. The cars were parked at an angle with their fronts aimed at the curbs. Dad was driving slowly down the main street, and some people even waved. The sun was beaming its warmth and so were the people.

The redbrick buildings contrasted with the white siding on the other buildings. All the buildings had green shutters, if they had shutters. It was like driving into a postcard. Mom broke our concentration by reminding us to look forward as the incline of the street increased. The trees parted very slowly. It was like they were opening up a picture album and revealing its contents. As the picture was revealed, it opened to the size of the entire windshield. The road seemed to go right down into an expanse of water that was sparkling in the sun. It was as if the lake was covered in flashing lightbulbs which were all going off and on as we descended the hill. The farther down the hill we rode, the wider the lake became. This expanse of blue was placed right in the center of a valley with dark green, emerald-like hillsides shooting up from the edges of the water to touch the cotton, white clouds. Sailboats, motorboats, and fishing boats dotted the surface of the lake.

It almost seemed like God placed this spot—so it was not in plain sight. You had to know someone who had been here in order to find how to get here. It was gorgeous, and all of our mouths were hanging open with its beauty. Dad was just smiling, ear to ear, as he looked at us and heard our joy. He did not say anything. He did not have to.

He was happy because he was now where the "Musky" lived. I thought Musky was the name of a person. That was when Dad said he had to get his Musky license. I knew then that Musky were some kind of fish. The excitement just continued as we drove along. The road curved to the right as we reached the bottom of the hill. It followed the shoreline but was about ten feet above the water level.

We were driving down the west side of the lake. We could see the water constantly out the left side of the car. Some of the people had put wooden rafts out in the water. Dad said that they were anchored in place, and the people could swim and dive off of them.

We continued on our drive and came to the state fish hatchery. The state actually raised fish to put into the lake when they grew big enough. I counted eight ponds, which Dad said were for various kinds of fish to grow in. Each kind of fish had its own pond. We continued down the road. We came to a dirt road on the left as Dad slowed his car. Dad made the left turn on to the dirt road and slowly proceeded past a farmhouse and a small barn. The barn was covered with chicken wire. It was used to keep chickens penned in. Once we were past the barn, the trees started to cover over the road, and the dirt turned to a grass-covered pathway. We were now headed straight at the lake. The path was leading us to the back of a yellow house. The garage for one car was sticking out the back of the house on the right hand side. There was a small entry porch on the left side of the back of the house. Dad pulled the car up towards that porch. This would make it easier to unload the car. Dad had a key that he had received from Mr. Bailey. We all got out of the car and walked slowly over to the shade-covered porch. I continued to walk past the porch toward the water and the front of the house. There was a slight breeze from the lake. The view of the water and the smell brought to my nose by the breeze—were intoxicating. If this was great, what must the garden of Eden been like? I was so excited that I ran back to the porch which was painted dark brown. This contrasted with the yellow of the house but matched the trim. I ran up the steps and pulled open the screen door, which creaked as I opened it. Dad, Mom, and my sisters were all in the kitchen looking around. The white refrigerator contrasted with the dark green wall paint and the gray linoleum floor. We all walked into the dining and living area—which were combined. The dominating feature of this area was a brown furnace, which was four feet high and three feet wide. The floor was covered with dark green linoleum, and the walls were light green. The front of the room was a wall of windows, which looked out to the sunporch area. The sunporch looked out over the lake. The front screen door was in the center of the porch. It lined up perfectly with a stone pathway that led straight to a dock that went about fifty feet out into the lake. I noticed that a boat was tied to each side of the dock. The sun was streaming down through two, fifty-foot-tall maple trees. They threw their shade over two wooden Adirondack chairs. The chairs were placed on either side of the stone walkway.

My distraction caused by the beauty and wonder all around me was broken by Mom's voice calling me to help with the unloading of the car. We were always told to get the job done first, and then, we could explore. We brought all of the food into the kitchen first. Then, we brought in our suitcases and bedding. We set all of the suitcases at the base of the stairs which led to the second floor bedrooms. We finally went upstairs where we found three bedrooms. I noticed that the stairway was to the left of the furnace which was on the center of the back wall. To the left of the stairway was the bathroom that had no windows. It seemed that this place had everything—including the lake in the front yard.

Dad was very excited to be here but he never said those exact words. I knew he was anticipating the thrill of fishing. I didn't know that same thrill. Some things in life must be learned to be appreciated.

Mom said we would have lunch first, and then, we could enjoy the lake and outdoors. My sisters were not nearly as excited about the place as I was. Again, some things in life have to be learned to be appreciated. The water will do that to you.

Once we had finished lunch, we all went out to the front of the house and marveled at the lake. Mom was telling us about the dangers of the water and the dock. Dad was checking out his fishing tackle. I decided to watch what Dad was doing. I made sure that I did not distract him from his task. I had learned that Dad did not like to be asked a lot of questions. He wanted you to observe and learn. He knew all the answers—he just was not a talker. He said that the best learners were very good listeners. This caused me to pay close attention to what he was doing. He usually did things only once. This caused us to be fast learners.

I noticed that Dad had bought a new rod strictly for the musky fishing he did. I knew that I was not going to be touching that seven-foot rod. He had a huge reel on it, and I knew that it was extremely valuable. I never touched that rod for years. I knew he always wanted the right tools to get the job done. These were his musky fishing tools. He never actually told me not to touch them, I just thought that it would be better not to. I followed him as he got up from the chair. He carried his tackle down the dock and put it in the smaller boat of the two that were tied up. He already had his outboard motor mounted on the boat. The boat was all wood and had flat sides and a flat bottom. The sides were dark green, and it had red paint on the top of the sides. It had three boards inside which served as seats. They were gray. It was a very basic fishing boat for the time. I found out later that Mr. Bailey and his son-in-law built the boats themselves.

Dad got into the boat and started the engine. He let it warm up as he organized the fishing rods and equipment in the boat. The smell of that blue smoke from the motor combined with the smell of the lake permanently imprinted itself on the software of my brain. Whenever I get that smell, I still have the warmth of joy come all over me.

Dad told me to push the boat away from the dock. I sat down on the dock and put my feet against the side of the boat and pushed it away from the dock. Dad gave the motor a little gas and told me to tell Mom he would be back at suppertime. It was one o'clock, and he had to fish. He was doing what was most enjoyable to him. I stood on the dock as he motored out to the deeper water where he said the musky lived.

Mom's voice filled the air as she called us to the sunporch to play scrabble. It was sunny and warm, and the scent of huge pine trees mixed with the scent of the lake. I just wanted to be outdoors. Mom said, "We were here to relax, so calm down." She handed me some Superman comic books, so that really helped. The scents of the outdoors and the lapping of the water against the cement break wall did have a relaxing effect. I probably would not have noticed them if I had not calmed down—then Mom said it was time to take a nap. I did not want to calm that much. There was too much to see and do. I slowly proceeded up the stairs to my bedroom. The window in my room was open. A screen kept the bugs out but not all the sounds coming from the outdoors, especially the sounds of the water. I just lay in bed that afternoon. I could not relax and sleep: the birds singing, the warmth of the sun, the sounds of the boat motors, and the smell of the lake—were just too much. It was the longest forty-five minutes of the day. I went down the stairs quietly and headed for the sunporch. I sat on a chair and watched the boats and the fisherman. The afternoon sun was shining across the lake and hitting the dark green hillside which rose up out of the water and touched the powder blue sky. I looked closer, and it seemed like the hillside was finger-painted in various hues of green. The white sailboats on the surface of the lake looked like pieces of bright white paper being blown around by the breath of God. I have loved Chautauqua Lake ever since that day.

I saw a dark green boat coming towards our side of the lake. As it got closer, I could see it was Dad. I walked out of the sunporch and down to the end of the dock, and there, I waited quietly. As Dad approached the dock, he turned the boat so that the bow was pointing out to the center of the lake. The boat was parallel to the dock and about five feet away. He threw me a rope and said, "Hold it." The boat's momentum put it right up against the dock. Dad got out of the boat to tie the stern to a dock post, and then, he walked to me at the bow and said, "Always tie a boat up like this." As he tied the rope, I watched very closely. When he was done, he just walked down the dock toward the house. I did not ask anything of him until we were on the shore. I asked if he had any action out there. He said he thought he had a hit, but that was about it. Then he explained that the musky is the "lion" of the freshwater. It takes a long time to catch one. Catching one was one of his goals. As we walked the stone path, Mom called us for supper through the screen door of the sunporch. I thought the day had flown by.

After we had supper, Dad was getting itchy again. You could see it. He played around with Anne and Becky for a while, and then, he announced that he was going after his musky that evening. Hearing him talk about it got me excited about fishing. He was giving me a little bit of the fishing infection. Dad headed for the dock and the boat. I watched him motor out to the deeper water and out of our sight. The sun was just ready to dip below the horizon when Dad returned from his evening musky run. As he turned the boat parallel to the dock, he told me that if he had running lights on the boat, he would have stayed out another hour because they were hitting. Dad worked hard at all he did. He had a huge grin on his face as he bent down and reached under the seat of the boat. When he stood up, he was holding a thirty-eight-inch-long Musky. He was very happy. Now, he really had the fever. He reminded meet that he had four tags left. That meant he could catch four more Musky.

The house was all aglow that evening. Dad was seated outside talking with Mr. Bailey and some other men. They wanted to know where he caught the musky and what he was using for bait. I was trying to listen to the conversation while taking part in the scrabble game on the sunporch. The excitement tapered off, and we were all tired and ready for bed.

Dad was up before anyone, and he was out in the lake looking to catch number two. He returned at about eleven o'clock. He announced that tomorrow was the 4th of July, and then, he reached in his pocket and took out a firecracker. He lit it with his cigarette and threw it out over the water. The bang was heard all over, but he threw two more just to make sure. He always loved the 4th because he was a veteran of World War II and knew firsthand what the 4th was all about. He infected me with that same love. He said that we were in a special place this day, this summer. I wondered what he meant. I knew if I asked what he meant he would just tell me to wait and see. He always said that patience had to be learned.

The next day arrived. It was a beautiful, sunny 4th of July. In every once in a while, you could hear some firecrackers banging. After supper that evening, Dad did not go fishing. He was answering the sound of the firecrackers with his own. More and more bangs could be heard as the sun fell beneath the horizon. Mr. and Mrs. Bailey were now sitting by the water in their chairs. Mr. Bailey explained the procedures for the 4th to Dad but I could not hear it. Dad walked to his car and returned with his arms full of long red sticks. I figured out that they were red flares.

I did not ask what they were for because that was not our way—watch, listen, and learn was our way. Mom would remind us of that often.

The sun was gone and in its place was a purple-colored horizon that rose above the green hillsides surrounding the lake. The sky was becoming darker and darker as the moon had started to glow on the surface of the lake. The green, red, and white lights of the boats were moving across the water. The sights and sounds were glorious. But sometimes, clouds of smoke and the smell of sulphur in the air covered them. A slight breeze cleared the smoke, and all was suddenly quiet. It was as if everyone heard the word "Stop" at the same time. Dad went over to his chair and pulled the red flares out from under it. He carried them out on to the dock and stuck a flare on top of each of the four dock posts. He looked at his watch as Mr. Bailey said to light them at ten o'clock. About ten minutes later, Dad walked back out and lit all four flares. What happened next was just unique and wonderful.

The red flares on our dock overcame the darkness of the night. Every dock had red flares all around the circumference of the lake. It was like a giant wall switch was flicked on, and all the red lights came on. It had to have a mysterious and beautiful look from an airplane. It all lasted for about thirty minutes, and it was done except for the sulphur-laden air. The slight breeze swept the odor from our nostrils but not our minds.

The fireflies had the night back to themselves. They seemed to glow much brighter before the flares were lit. As the smoke cleared, so did our eyes. The fireflies became brighter, and the crickets and tree toads were back in the noise business. They were all signaling that it was time to go to bed. My sisters and I started to walk the short stone path to the sun porch which glowed with its yellow light. Dad said goodnight as he sat back in an Adirondack chair and gazed at the last remaining lights on the lake. Mom escorted us to the house and made sure we brushed our teeth and said our prayers. It had been a very full and exciting day. I lied in bed hearing Dad's voice outside and all the night sounds, as a breeze came over my face and closed my eyes.

When my eyes opened, I could hear the lapping of the water on the break wall and the boat motors running. A very cool breeze came in the window but could not beat the sunshine in the race to enter the room. I looked out the window at the diamond-covered lake. I could see that Dad's boat was gone. He had already left to get the big one. I slowly put my slippers on and headed down the stairs. The house was in the shade and stayed very cool in the morning. The second floor usually became very warm in the evening. The first floor always stayed very cool and this morning, it was very crisp. I made a left turn from the staircase and walked around the furnace and headed for the kitchen. I opened the cupboard where Mom put the cereal and got out the rice krispies for breakfast. I sat down at the kitchen table and turned the box of cereal to read the back. I was enticed to send in my quarter and the box top to receive a small atomic submarine. It could dive and surface in the bathtub. I remembered I was at the lake, and I could order this when I got home. I finished my cereal and walked to the sink to rinse out my bowl. The sun was pouring in the kitchen window and telling me to go to the front sunporch. As I stepped into the sun porch, the glints of sunlight on the surface of the lake took my breath away. They seemed to be jumping from ripple to ripple across the surface. Dad's boat was already gone but he had left one of his tackle boxes right next to one of the Adirondack lawn chairs. Mom, Becky, and Anne had come down the stairs as I was about to go up and get dressed. I ran back down the stairs after dressing and asked Mom if I could go outside. She said I could. I went out and sat down in the chair next to Dad's tackle box. I could not resist the temptation. I opened the box and saw an astounding assortment of lures and fishing supplies. This was the equipment Dad used to fish for bass and walleye. Two of the lures caught my eye. I took them out of the tackle box and set them on the cement break wall. I went and got my fishing rod and sat back down in the chair. I hooked one of the lures to the snap swivel on my line. I knew in my heart I was doing the wrong thing, and yet, I kept going down this wrong path. I stood up and walked over to the break wall. I proceeded to begin casting from the shoreline over and over.

A rowboat was tied up at the dock and was straight out from the break wall. I was casting into the water to the right of the rowboat. On a cast, the lure went straight into the rowboat and broke in two pieces. One piece stayed on my line, and the other fell in the boat somewhere. The feeling of excitement of using the lure turned to terror in that instant. I had taken two of Dad's lures without permission, and on top of that, I had broken one of them. I knew I was in for it when Dad got back. The real problem was that I knew I deserved whatever he decided to do to me.

Dad returned at about one o'clock that afternoon. He stepped off the dock and headed straight for his tackle box. I stood on the sunporch and watched as he opened the tackle box. It was just a matter of minutes, and he closed it up. He stood up and looked out at the lake. Then, he began to slowly walk out on the dock. He was looking all around when he focused on the rowboat. It was as if the rowboat was calling to him. I turned and headed for the bathroom at that very moment. I could not face the truth, but I was about to have no choice. As I was stepping out of the bathroom, Dad's voice was calling for me to come to the sun porch. I entered the sun porch, and he looked at me and asked if I had taken a lure from his tackle box. I told him no. I was astounded at my own lips. Why did I lie? Dad looked at me and said that he had found a broken lure in the rowboat. Mom said she saw me doing some casting from the shore. He knew that I had taken the lure. He said that because I had lied I would be grounded to the house for the rest of this day and the next. What really upset me was that I had ruined the trust that Dad had in me. I ran up the stairs to the bedroom, lied down, and cried because of my foolishness. I admitted to my lie—but the damage was done. I would have to rebuild my word and the trust of Dad's eyes, and that would take a long time.

The next day was spent looking outside and reading. I thought about what I had done and why I did it. There was no answer. I only knew I was not going to lie to Dad again.

Outside the day was sunny and bright, and it progressed very slowly. I could not and did not complain. Every moment told me that telling the truth was best.

Dad came in from his evening fishing run and walked off of the dock and sat down in one of the Adirondack chairs. He was just relaxing and looking out at the calm waters of the lake. I could see him from the sunporch. I was reading one of my comic books when I heard him come up the porch steps. The screen door squeaked as he pushed it open and walked into the brightly lit sunporch. It was a warm night, and the fireflies were out. We turned out the porch lights and watched them. After a while, Dad turned one of the lights back on. He stood up and asked if I wanted to go musky fishing with him in the morning. I did not hesitate in accepting the invitation. I was truly excited to take part in Dad's favorite pastime. I wanted to be with him and learn how to hunt the "lion of the freshwater." He said he would set me up with the proper equipment in the morning. I felt that I was in this dark valley. Dad's invitation was showing me the way out of that darkness. I wasn't able to sleep well that night because of my excitement.

When I awoke, Dad was calling my name as he stuck his head into my room through the open doorway. The morning had a slight chill in the air. I really felt it when my feet hit the floor. I put my socks on immediately. I put my long pants on and headed down the stairs. I turned the corner for the kitchen. Dad was coming out of the kitchen with a baseball hat in his hand. He told me I would need it because the sun was very intense this morning. I followed as he walked out to the sunporch. He opened the screen door and proceeded down the steps to the stone pathway. I was right behind him as his feet hit the dock. I looked up at the oak and maple tree branches. It seemed like they were stretching their branches as they awoke to the morning sun. The smell of the oak and pine trees and lake combined in the air and entered my nostrils. The scent caused my heart to remind my brain of the joy of being here with my Dad. The bright sunlight caused our two shadows to hit the dock together just as our feet did the same thing. We walked down the dock and stepped into the dark green boat with its red top edges. Dad went to the back of the boat and started the outboard motor. I thought the smell of the exhaust and the water was like cologne. The odor was imprinted on my brain. It was to be remembered forever to remind me of a joyous time with Dad. We untied the boat and pushed it out from the dock. The motor had warmed up, and Dad motored us out to the center of the lake. The sun heating up the air, and its brightness caused the jewels on the surface of the water to sparkle. The green-velvet-covered hills that surrounded the lake seemed to roll the edges of the velvet right into the lake.

As the sun rose higher in the sky, the jewels disappeared revealing a dark blue-green expanse of water. We were at the center of the lake. Dad handed me a fishing rod and explained how we were going to troll along the edges of the weed beds in the lake. That was when he told me, "The Lion of the lake likes to wait in the weeds. When a fish comes swimming by, the lion pounces from the weeds and eats its prey." Now I understood why the musky is called the "lion of freshwater."

The lures we were using looked like fish that were about eight to ten inches in length, and they weighed as much as the bluegills I had caught. Dad attached the lure to a two-foot-long ladder made of steel which was tied to my line. The steel was so musky could not bite off my line. Their teeth were extremely sharp. This was serious fishing like I had not known before. We were about to enter the hunt!

Dad told me to throw the lure into the water and let the line out. The motor was moving us along at about four miles an hour. This in itself caused the line to go out. I think I let out a hundred and fifty feet of line before I stopped. Dad did the same with his lure. The tips of our rods began to vibrate with the action of the lures which were now close to the bottom of the lake. We were trolling for about two hours when the tip of my rod stopped vibrating and began to bend toward the water. Dad said, "Give it a hard jerk." I did and then felt a hard jerk back. Dad read the look on my face and said, "Keep the line taught and reel him in." Those last two words were the most exciting. Dad shut off the motor and reeled his line in just in case I needed help. I saw the white belly of the fish roll over as it got up near the boat. That was when Dad said that it was a gar pike. It looked like some kind of prehistoric fish. It had a six-inch-long bill—almost like a swordfish's. The bill was lined with teeth but did not come to a point. The body was like a musky. It certainly looked strange. Dad said that they ate what the muskies ate. He never heard of them ever hurting a person. I did not know such creature existed. Dad unhooked him and threw him back. Dad said, "He was about thirty five inches long, but we do not want him."

The sun was now very high in the sky, and we were both hungry. We reeled in our lines and headed to the shore and the house for our lunch. As we were riding back, I thought how Dad approached his hobby with the same discipline he used at work. He loved fishing, and his time on the water was joyful, quiet, and a good time for meditating.

Mom had tuna fish sandwiches waiting for us when we got to the kitchen table. We ate our food and really had little conversation. When we were done, Dad said he was going to walk up to Mr. Bailey's house and find out where all the muskies were hiding. He was gone for an hour or so. I knew he was going to find out some musky secrets from the old man. I decided to read a Batman comic book while I sat out at the water's edge. The day had become hot and humid—as a summer day should be.

Dad had forgiven my foolish lie, but now, I had to forgive myself for my failure. I had lots of time to think while we were out in the boat trolling. Now, I was sitting by the water in a chair. It looked like I was reading a science book, but I was thinking again. Dad returned from his talk with Mr. Bailey and sat down in the chair next to me. He pulled his tackle box over to the chair and opened it while he asked if I wanted to go out fishing with him after dinner. I did not hesitate to say yes. That afternoon slowly turned into a beautiful, amber-colored evening. I was giving up watching the "event," as we came to call it, to really go fishing with Dad. The event happened every evening at six thirty. I knew that my fishing invitation did not happen every night. I had to take advantage of Dad's invitation now.

We headed for the dock after dinner. Dad checked out all of his equipment after he had started the motor. He was warming it up as he always did. I relaxed as the motor warmed and inhaled the scent of the water mixed with the exhaust fumes. The aroma almost put me in a trance of thought. The water was already putting my mind into deep thought. Dad blurted out, "Push us off." It brought me back to the moment, and I did what he asked. We motored out to the edge of the weed bed and dropped our lines in. We began to make our slow troll as the waves were shrinking to the size of ripples.

The sun was almost ready to dip behind the hills surrounding the lake when it happened. I felt a very quick but heavy pull on my rod. The rod was bending over immediately. Dad stopped the motor and asked if it felt like a fish. I said, "I think it is, but now, it feels like weeds." He was already into the drill. He knew it was a fish. There's no substitute for experience. He said, "Reel him in." As I reeled him in, the jerks became very strong and violent. Dad said, "He probably got a glimpse of the boat." Once the fish was up next to the boat, Dad netted him and brought him into the boat. We both sat down and took a breath. I had caught my first musky. Dad said, "Most people can fish for days, or even weeks, and not get a Musky." He was almost as excited as I was. He proceeded to step on the fish's head to hold it while he measured it. He pronounced it long enough to keep. That meant it was legal to keep. Dad reached for the bat and hit the fish in the head twice. He did not want it flipping around in the boat and biting us with its barracuda-like teeth. He sat down and headed the boat to the house. We were tying up the boat as the sun dipped behind the velvet-covered hills and left its purple ribbon just above the hilltops. As we walked the dock to the lake house, Dad held the musky up for all to see. The porch screen door slammed shut just as Mom's foot hit the stone walkway. She walked quickly to the dock. Dad just said, "Shhhhh. Todge caught it." They were both smiling. Then, I remembered my Dad's forgiveness. I am very grateful for second chances. The glory only lasted a few minutes.

Dad went right to work, and he cleaned and prepared the fish for the freezer. Mom said she was looking forward to tomorrow night's dinner.

I got up the next morning to a glorious, warm day. It was a day full of swimming and fishing for bluegills and sunfish. They were a long way from musky fishing but was still fun. Dad said I could use the rowboat to fish along the shoreline for bass. I did that exactly. I felt more like a fisherman after the other night's experience. I rowed about a hundred yards down the shoreline and saw a patch of lily pads. I fished there for half an hour and found out I could catch more fish off of the dock. I rowed back to the dock where I found my sister Anne wanting to get into the boat. Dad had just tied up his boat and was sitting in a chair watching. Anne was demanding to get into the rowboat. I just got close to the dock, and she jumped into the boat. She told me that it was her turn to row. We switched seats, and she very quickly had her fill of rowing. Dad's chair was up close to the cement break wall which ran along the shoreline. Anne said she wanted to get out of the boat in front of Dad. I proceeded to back the transom of the boat up to the flat surface of the break wall. Dad already had a huge grin on his face. It was like he knew what was about to happen.

Anne was becoming more assertive in her requests to get out of the boat. She did not want me to dock the boat. She was getting out in front of Dad!

I was rowing harder to get the back of the boat up against the break wall, and then, she could step right out on the top of the break wall. The transom of the boat was about three feet from the break wall when Anne stood up on the backseat to grab a steel loop sticking out of the top of the break wall right in front of Dad. The loop of steel was there to tie a rope to. Anne's little fingers were wrapped tightly around the curved steel rod. Her feet were still in the boat. Dad's grin became much bigger. Mom was sitting next to Dad when she said, "Chick." And then, Dad just said, "Mother, let Anne learn." I was now rowing furiously to get the transom up against the cement. Anne was pushing the boat back out away from the cement with her feet. She was winning. Dad was now laughing out loud. I was splashing the oars as I furiously rowed, and Anne was all stretched out over the water between the boat and the cement—screaming orders at me. She kept lunging with her legs and just pushed the boat farther away from the wall. Dad was now belly laughing at the sight. She was screaming for me to row harder. The water was flying everywhere while her body was stretching to its limit. I had reached my physical limit and stopped rowing at the very instant she gave her last lunge. Her legs dropped into the one-foot-deep water as she screamed, "You jerk!" Dad just reached over the break wall and pulled Anne out of the shallow water and up onto the grass. She was crying but was still able to look over at me and yell "You jerk!" at me one more time. I was exhausted as I tied up the rowboat, but I could not keep from laughing. Dad was wiping away the tears of laughter as Mom escorted Anne to the lake house for a change of clothes. Mom just turned to Dad once and grinned. Mr. Bailey said it was one of the best comedy routines he had ever seen. A great time was had by all that afternoon. Anne was cured of going in the boat with me. I was really looking forward to the "event" this evening. It was the perfect ending for a perfect day.

At six thirty in the evening, the man who lived about four docks to the left of our dock would walk out his front door. He would stand and look at the water for a moment, and then, he would walk out onto his dock. My friends and I would stand on the shoreline watching him. He was very consistent and meticulous. His dock was a freshly painted white, and his house was bright white with red shutters.

Mr. Lutz walked down his dock and unsnapped the cover of his boat, just enough for him to climb into it. He turned the key to start it. The boat would always break the silence of the amber and red evening with a loud, deep rumble of power. Mr. Lutz would back off the throttle to a very smooth idle speed. He then continued to unsnap the rest of the boat cover as the engine warmed. He was never hurried in his actions. His boat was always spotless and glistened in the evening glow. It was a twenty-two-foot-long, mahogany Chris-Craft runabout. Its reddish brown color was enhanced by its copper bottom paint and tan interior. Mr. Lutz always made sure that the American flag flew on the stern, and the Chris-Craft flag was on the bow. He folded the cover neatly and placed it on the dock. Then he backed the throttle off of the fast idle speed. He untied the ropes and pushed the boat away from the dock. A soft clunk could be heard as he engaged the propeller. The engine labored as the boat began to move slowly and slip out into the lake. He always took it out of gear and engaged reverse to the get the weeds off of the propeller about three hundred yards from shore. The transom and its exhaust pipes were aimed right at us as we watched from the shore. We would all count from one to three and hear the clunk, as the boat was put into forward gear again. Mr. Lutz would give the boat a half throttle, and once it was on plane, he would give it full throttle. The deep roar of power was music to our ears as we watched the smoothness of the vision disappear from sight. We could still hear that magnificent sound long after he was out of sight.

The man did every activity with flow and grace. It all had a pattern. He showed class and purpose in his every move. He never looked to see us watching and was never a show off. He simply showed an appreciation for his equipment. As we watched night after night, we all had the feeling that he knew he was blessed, and he took care of what he was blessed with.

I never met Mr. Lutz. I would not even know his face if he walked by us—but he was an example of stewardship to all of us. You could depend on his consistent behavior. If more people were like him, this would be quite a place to live. He was class in action. It was his life not an act.

The lake seemed like a learning center without telling you that you were being taught. I had two weeks of classes every July. I learned the power of truth and trust. I felt the love of family and saw what gave my Dad great pleasure. I learned how to handle a boat, how to swim, and I established the foundation for the love of fishing and the outdoors. I was exposed to great wealth and the people who had it and found them to be generous. All of this was possible because of the relationships that Dad had nurtured in his life.

Go West, Young Man

I had spent all of my thirteen years of life in a small town. It was not a bad thing. Everyone in my small town knew me even if I did not know them. The fact that I felt it was my small town was very important. I had a real sense of belongingness while still not knowing my place in the scheme of life. The doors of our house were seldom locked, and a stranger was recognized as a stranger immediately. Everyone had a purpose in our town. It seemed normal to be useful. My first venture out of my state was about to open my eyes to a giant world.

Dad had an older brother named Tony. Dad had told me that when they were young boys, he and Tony had decided to take a swim in Eighteen Mile Creek. Tony had taken in a lot of water and went under. He almost drowned on that day. Dad did not go into the details, but Tony survived. Tony had a breathing problem from that point on. The doctors said that the water had contributed to Tony having asthma attacks. The family was advised that the best thing for Tony was to move out to Colorado. The air was much drier out in the West. Eventually, Tony did move to Denver, Colorado. Dad said that it did help his breathing tremendously. Uncle Tony married Aunt Helen, and they had three boys in their family. I thought that it would be exciting to have brothers. I was only thinking of the positive aspects. You could have your own ball team and a family gang of protection. I did not think of the different ages, and that it does not work that way. I later found that out by observing Uncle Tony's boys and other families.

I had my sisters, and it was working just great most of the time. I loved them, and they loved me. We all have our own ways of showing it. The trick was to recognize their ways of showing it.

I was getting ready to be a big shot freshman in high school in the fall.

One night, Dad was smiling at the dinner table when Mom announced that we would be taking a trip out to Colorado to see Uncle Tony and Aunt Helen this summer. It really did not register with me. I just nodded in approval like I had seen Dad do so many times. Anne and Becky did not say anything either. I knew it would take more discussion and information for us to appreciate the scope of this trip. Mom told Dad one evening that she had talked to some of her relatives in Iowa. They told her we could stay there for a few days on the way out to Colorado. I was listening to their conversation when it hit me that this was going to be a very long drive. I got out the encyclopedia to find out the distance from our house to Littleton, Colorado. It was around four thousand miles. I was shocked on the actual distance. I thought that Colorado was on the other side of the world when I estimated the distance. We were actually going to do this. I asked Mom how long it would take to get there. She said about a week, maybe more. She said that Dad was taking a three-week vacation. I was speechless. Dad only took vacations to go fishing. This was a very special vacation. Besides, I found out we would be closer to Roy Rogers and the Air Force Academy. This truly could be a very exciting trip.

The weather was growing warmer each day, and the school year was over. I had my own small suitcase, and we were all thinking about the travel. This was definitely a different thinking in our family. Every time we mentioned the amount of miles to someone, I winced at the thought. I decided to forget the number—that made the distance easier to handle.

The morning of departure finally arrived. Dad had made sure that his Ford station wagon was ready for the trip. He had new tires on it, and all of the brakes were new. All of the fluids were topped off. The workhorse was ready for the long haul.

We left our home in North Evans and proceeded to head west. Dad drove that car for more than twelve hours that first day. We were long past Chicago and had actually gone more than six hundred miles. Dad was very happy at achieving that first leg of the trip. It was very dark, and Dad and Mom decided we needed to find a room for the night. Dad was visibly tired from the driving. He finally found a motel that had a room. Dad and Mom slept in one bed, and my sisters slept in the other bed. I had a cot to sleep on, and I was grateful. I also had permission to watch some of the summer Olympics on the TV in the room—only if I kept the sound down. I thought that was really cool. I watched them for about an hour, and then, I had to turn it off because I kept fading off myself. This was my first time in a motel. It was hard to stay asleep, but we were together and safe.

The room was chilly when we awoke in the morning. The night just seemed to pass so quickly. Dad was already up and out to the car to get some milk out of the cooler for our cereal. He opened the door to come into the room, and the bright morning sunshine swept across the room for just an instant. It was followed by a puff of cold air from the outside. Once we finished our food, we all pitched in and helped in loading the car. I could see the mist from the green-covered land as the car was being prepared for the next leg of the trip. Dad verbalized his satisfaction with the number of miles covered on the first day. It must have been seven o'clock when we left.

As we were riding toward the center of our country, Dad said that the land was becoming flatter. We were heading toward the plain area of the country. It was also time for our peanut butter and jelly sandwiches which Mom had made when we were back at the motel that morning. I asked Dad what our destination was for that day. The answer was Sioux Falls, Iowa.

We were all "eating on the fly." That was what Dad would say—meaning that we were not stopping the car. It just seemed to add to the adventure. As Dad drove, he would point to a unique motel. Some had what looked like teepees for rooms, and some had rocket ships for the main office. There was always something different in their designs to get you to stop, look, and then stay. They did not get my Dad to stop because he was on a mission.

We arrived in Iowa and pulled into the driveway of a freshly built ranch-style house. It had four bedrooms and was very big and nice as far as we were concerned. The owners were Mom's cousins. They came out to greet us as we got out of the car. They were very gracious and kind, and they said that we could stay for a couple nights. In fact, we had to stay because they had invited all of their family to come to a picnic and meet their relatives from New York. The next evening, they had their picnic in the backyard of their home. I learned that they owned a very large farm outside of town. Mom's dad was a farmer, and here were his relatives whom he had never met, and they are farmers. I thought that was very interesting. Mom was asking all kinds of family questions and just talking up a storm. She was excited. I just wanted to get on the road to Uncle Tony's house in Denver. My wish was fulfilled the following morning as we said our good-byes.

I wanted to meet the man who made the lamp I received for Christmas a few years before. It was made from a cedar tree. The lamp was an inverted Y shape. Through the center was a fence carved out of cedar. On the fence was a real leather saddle. It was a miniature saddle, of course. The inverted Y was attached to a crosscut piece of a twelve-inch-diameter cedar. All around the edges, the initials TM were burned into the wood. They were done in many different styles and designs. I thought it was unique and beautiful. Uncle Tony did it all. I wanted to meet the person who would take the time to do this for me. I wanted to give him my thanks. I felt a connection and wanted it completed in real life. I thought of this as we drove through the Badlands of the Dakotas and observed the twisted, windblown trees.

Dad and Mom broke my thoughts as they told us all about some of the criminals who would hide out in this truly, desolate place. Many of my cowboy stories would refer to this place, and now, I was in it. It generated quite a unique feeling. I was seeing this place in the bright sunlight. There were a lot of oddly shaped towers of rock and very jagged cliffs. They formed some spooky shadows in the sunlight of day. They must really be scary at night. It was no wonder that the criminals wanted to live there because no one wanted to go looking for them in this place. Anne and Becky thought it was not a nice place to be. They both had concerned looks on their faces. That concern changed as we left that area and proceeded to Mount Rushmore. Seeing the presidents' faces in the sunlight was very comforting. It was truly an awesome sight to behold.

We left and were now headed to Denver. The land was becoming far flatter, and the hills were becoming rolling plains of grass. Dad was definitely making his way west.

I thought of all the Westerners I had seen on TV and how they traveled for weeks. We certainly had it good compared to the people of long ago. The sun had gone down, and it was ten o'clock at night. I was in the front seat with Dad, and I told him that I had to go to the bathroom. I knew what his solution was going to be. He slowed down and pulled off to the side of the road. It was extremely dark because there was cloud covering the sky, and there were no street lights. Dad turned off the car motor, and with it, he turned off the lights. He told me it was okay to get out. I got out of the car and took about three steps away from the car. I was actually scared so it took some time to relax and go. Dad must have been aware of my tension because he never tried to hurry me. I ran those three steps to the car and jumped in when I was done. Dad started the car just as I closed the door.

He hit the lights, and I looked up and out of the car at the same instant. All I saw were yellow eyes glowing all around the car. Fear was running all through and around my body as I realized I had been out among those eyes. My eyes were moving so fast that I did not allow them to focus on any one thing. Buffalo surrounded us. All I could think was that if one of them had rubbed up against me when I was out of the car, I would have screamed. The result would have been a stampede, and my family and I would have been killed. My mouth was wide open but very dry. That was when Dad said that it was a good thing that an electric fence was in place. I finally focused, and there it was. I had so much terror that I didn't notice we were protected. That also explained the slight grin on his face as he pulled the car slowly on to the pavement and began to accelerate. My sister Becky woke up and saw what I saw. She must have felt the same way because she was softly crying while Mom held her and said everything was all right. As Dad got the car back up to speed, he stated that we were stopping at the next motel we see. I just looked straight ahead and softly said, "Good!"

I think I had watched too many westerns. The buffalo were not free to roam anymore. That was the topic of conversation as we all fell asleep in our motel room. It had to be explained to Anne because she slept through the whole episode. I just wanted the light of day to come quickly.

Morning came, and as we ate our cereal, I knew we would be in Denver this day. That was excitement enough to get us all moving. The sunlight poured into the motel room when Dad opened the door. The air was chilly, but the sun brought its visual promise of warmth. We were just over the border of Colorado, and the humidity of the east was gone.

We were back on the road, and the light of day revealed that we were in a different land. You could see this endless piece of gray ribbon laid on top of a green carpet in God's family room. The ribbon stretched perfectly straight for miles, and then, it would curve ever so slightly. The stripes on the road glowed white under the sun. There were no guardrails and houses for miles. The power lines would appear and disappear, and sometimes, a route sign sprang into view at an intersection. This must have been what the Lone Ranger called "the open range." There were no power lines back then and no fences of any kind.

We started up an incline in the road for about two miles, and as we crested the top of the rise, you could literally see for miles. The view took my breath away. It was a glistening city many miles ahead. The backdrop for the city was the snow-capped Rocky Mountains and a shimmering, sun-filled blue sky. It was like a model city being unveiled at a home show. The sun was brighter than I had ever seen. Dad said it was because of the dry air, and the fact that we were almost a mile above sea level. It was an astounding sight. This was why uncle Tony moved here.

All of a sudden, the two-lane highway turned into an expressway. Anne, Becky, and I were looking at all the new sights, and before you knew it, we were on the other side of the city heading out of town. Mom said that we had missed the Littleton exit. Dad got us all turned back around and headed in the right direction. We got off at the correct exit. We were in Uncle Tony's town. The trip was not completed until we pulled into the driveway of a newer, three-bedroom, ranch style home. I wondered if this was the right one. Then Uncle Tony and Aunt Helen came walking out of the front door to greet us. We all took a deep breath at the same time. Mom just said, "We made it."

Uncle Tony and Aunt Helen's three boys—Stephen, Tommy, and Mark—followed them out of the front door. Uncle Tony approached Dad and shook his hand, and then, he said, "Welcome to Denver." You could see that they were brothers because they both had the same headshake when they acknowledged something or someone. They were brothers for all to see. It was neat to see them together.

The sleeping arrangements were all made as we unpacked the car. I must say that I did not care where I was sleeping because we were finally in Denver, and that was all that counted.

The excitement continued because we were going out to a real restaurant for dinner. We had been to hotdog stands but never an actual restaurant. I thought we had hit big time. When we walked into the restaurant, we were on our best behavior. My sisters and I didn't say a word unless we were spoken to. The waiter came and took our order. I had fried chicken and Texas toast. I had never even heard of a Texas toast before. Anne's and Becky's eyes were as big as mine. We were watching all that was going on. It was a unique and wonderful thing to be waited on. Uncle Tony said we would love this place, and he was right. I was hoping we would do this every night. That was not on the schedule. We went back to the house and settled down to the news at nine o'clock. That sure did feel strange. We were so used to the eleven o'clock news. It threw my internal clock off. That was when we were reminded that we were on Rocky Mountain. All these changes made the trip more exciting. It was nice to go to bed knowing that tomorrow could be more exciting than today. We were in the middle of making memories for life.

I awoke the next morning to an extremely bright, sunny day. The sky was a very blue, and the air was very dry. There was not one cloud in the sky. It was way too nice to be inside, so I played catch with my cousin Stephen. It did not take long before we had a ball game going in the backyard. My cousins loved playing baseball. We broke for a lunch of good old peanut butter and jelly sandwiches. That was when I found out we were going swimming that afternoon. We were going to the community pool.

Once we were there, I jumped into the pool right away because I thought it was a rather hot day. The air temperature was in the high eighties, so the water felt very comfortable. The shock was after I got out of the water. It was cold. How could that be? Then it was explained that the water evaporated off of my body so fast that it literally took the heat from my body with it. This was all because the air was so dry. It was surprising when the air temperature was so high. I did not need a towel because I was dry in a matter of minutes. Once I was dry, everything was back to normal. Well, not really, because then, I noticed that we certainly did not seem to sweat as much either. Actually, we did, but it evaporated so quickly you were never sticky like back home. We headed back to Uncle Tony's house for a hotdog roast that evening. Mom said that this clean air made us hungrier. I was thinking that the food would even taste better. Those hotdogs tasted like steak. We were really enjoying our stay very much.

The next day we got up, we were informed that we were going to a silver mine. I could never have imagined that I would be in silver mine. I saw so many of them blown up by dynamites on the westerns. We drove about an hour and joined a tour with the light helmets on our heads. We were only allowed so far, and that was fine with me because I did not want to be inside a cave. I laughed at myself because this was a tourist attraction. We were all very safe. When we were done, Uncle Tony said, "We were going to a special restaurant on top of a mountain."

We were in our car riding to this mountain, and it was a bright sunny day, but as we approached the base of the mountain, it very quickly turned cloudy. The road we were on was up one side of the mountain and twisted back and forth up the side. We were always on the edge, or so it seemed. This tension sure did add to the adventure. As we drove up the side, we were getting closer to the clouds. Dad was definitely taking his time. We finally made it to the top. Uncle Tony said, "You are now on top of Mount Evans." It really hit me because I grew up in North Evans, New York. We got out of the car, and there was a plaque explaining how this was the highest point in Colorado and the history of the area. The sky was gray and cloudy it almost said out loud, "I am ready to snow on you." There was a stiff, cold breeze blowing, but I was kept warm by the Air Force Academy sweatshirt Mom and

Dad bought at the gift shop by the silver mine. There was a gift shop and restaurant up here too. We entered the restaurant area.

We stood on a platform overlooking the dining area as we waited to be seated. I made sure I stood very straight and tall while I stuck my chest out. Someone would see the academy falcon on my chest and think I was going there. Some people said nice sweatshirt as they walked by. It worked! Mom saw me sticking my chest out. We were seated, and Mom made sure I was next to her. She explained what an honor it was to go to a military academy. She went on to explain how one had to qualify to be chosen. Arrogance was not one of the qualifications. I realized that my actions were very silly. I still enjoyed wearing the shirt, but now, it stood for something much greater than me. Mom also reminded me that Dad was in the United States Army Air Forces in World War II. It was now a privilege to wear that sweatshirt.

When we left that mountain top restaurant, my feet were back on the ground again. I stopped being puffed up, as Aunt Helen would say. She was very right.

That week in Denver was one of the fastest, action-packed weeks I had ever experienced in my life. We experienced family, restaurants, and tourism on a scale I never knew before. We actually saw the amber waves of grain and the purple mountains majesty. The song was never just a song after the trip. It was a visual verification of the beauty of America and the reasons why people sing and write of its beauty.

And the most important thing was the fact that Uncle Tony, Aunt Helen, Stephan, Tommy, and Mark were now real people. They were no longer names of people from a far off place. Uncle Tony and Aunt Helen had an addition to their family, just like we had my brother John, they had Anthony. His name was very appropriate.

They were all my beloved relatives from the western horizon. Because of this trip, I got to know them and America the beautiful.

Down on the Farm

Mom's parents lived in Palmyra, New York. Every summer, we would spend a week or two on the farms of either my grandparents or my mom's sister Aunt Isabel and her husband Uncle Clarence. I was always excited about this time away because we got to do things we would never normally do at home. At some point during our visit, we would stay a few nights with Grandma and Grandpa Pearson also.

It was about seven in the morning, and Grandpa told this six-year-old kid to get dressed, and I could go with him. He asked if I had any boots to wear, and Mom just said she brought them for me. She was thinking ahead to what would be happening during our stay. I put the boots on just as Grandpa said, "Come with me." I walked behind him staring at his coveralls and knee-high boots. I asked, "Where we were going?" He would just say, "You will see soon enough." He was a man of few words. As I followed him very closely, I noticed that his hands were very calloused and toughened. I just trusted him as we approached a small, barn-like structure. The building was faded red. The paint had been worn off by the weather. As we reached the building, he opened a door which was at the back of the building. The door had a carved, wooden handle with a metal thumb latch that you would push down to release the lock. Grandpa pushed on the door and stepped into the building. He waved for me to come along. As I entered, an odor entered my nostrils, and it was not pleasant.

An instant later, a huge noise entered my ears, and I forgot about the smell. Along with the sound came a strong breeze and dust and dirt flying up into the air. Grandpa turned around to look at me covering my face and had a giggle in his voice as he said, "They only make a fuss when a stranger enters." I took my hands down from my face just in time to see a chicken fly by the side of my head, screeching as she flew by. Her wings seemed to be flapping at a hundred miles an hour. She made a skid type landing about six feet in front of me. Grandpa held a deep, metal pan in his strong hands. It was filled with feed for the chickens. He explained how to correctly throw the feed out in front of you so that the birds would not surround you as you moved through the coup. He pulled another deep, metal dish from somewhere and handed it to me. As I reached and grabbed the dish, he put a big handful of his chicken feed into my pan. He reminded me not to bend down but to stand straight as you walk through the coup. He told me to be kingly when among any of God's creatures and humble around men.

One day, we went to the chicken coup and threw the feed, and Grandpa stopped and surveyed all the hens in the coup. He took two steps and grabbed a hen gently. He cradled the hen in his arm as we left the coup. I noticed that he still stroked the hen gently as we walked back towards the house. He circled around to the side of the house. I noticed a tree stump that was about three feet in diameter. He was heading right for it. I was puzzled but only for a moment. He laid the hen gently on its side on top of that stump. It seemed that his hand moved like lightning as he grabbed the hatchet that was stuck in the side of that stump, and in a single motion, he brought the cutting edge of that tool down on that hen's neck. The only sound I heard was the dull thud of the hatchet as it went through the neck and into the stump of wood. I was astounded to see the headless creature leap off of that stump and run around for about five seconds before it dropped over on its side. Grandpa very calmly walked over to the dead chicken and picked it up by the legs. He turned and just said it was nerves. I knew what he meant. He then proceeded to walk to the shed area of the house entrance and presented the bird to Grandma. She said, "Thank you Theodore." And she turned to walk through the screened door into the kitchen of the house.

Grandma was about five feet tall at most. She always seemed very elegant and proper in her mannerisms. Her white hair was always meticulously brushed and combed. Her dresses were never wrinkled or soiled, and she always stood very straight and proud. Her maiden name was Ford. That's correct! She knew what proper and elegant were because when she was growing up, she would visit the George Eastman house in Rochester, New York. Grandma's father owned an auto parts manufacturing company in the area, so she was around people of stature and accomplishment. She was never snooty. She was just very well-mannered woman and very respectful of others. I never heard her speak of an unkindly word about any other person.

After Grandma took the chicken from Grandpa, she took the bird to a table and began to pluck the feathers from its body. I know she used every part of that bird for some purpose. The meat was prepared for our dinner that night.

During a visit, about seven summers later, Mom told us we were going to Aunt Isabel's house. This was only about a fifteen-minute trip from Grandma's house. When we arrived, we had to go out, gather the milk cows, and get them into the barn. This was in preparation for the evening milking. Uncle Clarence and Aunt Isabel had automatic milking machines, but they would also milk some cows by hand. Mom wanted nothing to do with the cows. She did not trust them. I found out why. These animals are big and smart, and they wait for an opportunity to exert their presence on you. I watched as a cow pinned my cousin Harold against the cement wall of the barn with her side. He punched her in the head as hard as he could, and she backed off. He told me she was always trying to trap you because she was a nasty cow. He could not wait for her to get old. Then they would replace her with a kinder and more relaxed cow. I would not go near the cows until they were locked into their stanchions. This was a metal device which the cow had locked around their necks. The animal was free to move its head up and down, but the side-to-side movements were only inches. This really kept the cows in control. Sometimes, they would try to push you up against the four-foot-high walls that separated each cow. They figured out that they could still move their hindquarters and push you up against the short wall, but when you cracked them with a short two by four right across the rear, their respect returned. A thirteen-year-old was either crushed against the wall or fighting for their respect. All I wanted to do was to milk a cow and participate in the farm life.

Harold said to get a stool and a bucket and go over to Lady. I got the stool and a stainless steel bucket and looked for Lady. The names of some of the cows were above their stanchions on a piece of wood. They were not all named. The cows each had fresh straw to lie on in their compartments. Under the straw was the cement floor of the barn.

As you walked down the center of the barn, you saw cow rears on both sides because their heads were facing the outside walls. I found Lady and carefully stepped over the cement trough, which was about two feet behind Lady's rear hooves and right below her tail when she was standing. The trough was her bathroom. It was angled to flow to the door of the barn. Lady had a very gentle spirit, and that was why Harold said to milk her by hand. I placed the stool by her left side as I greeted her with a soft and warm voice. I placed my hand gently on her side and rubbed her side as I talked to her. Lady turned her head to see the source of this new voice, blinked her big, brown eye, and slowly turned her head forward again. I guess she was satisfied that I had good intentions. I sat down on the stool and slowly brought my hand down the fur of her side. I made sure my hands were warm. Those were Harold's instructions. He must have been watching because he appeared next to my stool and gave me some coaching as I tried to get the milking started. I found out it was not as easy as it looked. The barn cats knew I was going to stick with it because three of them sat down in a straight row waiting for their treat. They were about six feet away out in the center walkway of the barn. I was working very hard at trying to get the milk to squirt out, and it just would not happen.

Finally, I found the correct combination of finger tension and wrist action. That milk just shot into that bucket. I shot those cats with a straight stream of milk, about five times each. It was really funny to see their tongues come out and try and catch that stream of milk. The cats would throw their heads all over to catch every drop. The stream was so straight that it looked like a piece of string until it hit a cat in the head. They had their fill and slowly walked away. Lady turned to see me laughing. That big, brown eye seemed to say, "Hey, are you done yet?" I got her message. She was running out of patience. I picked up my half-full bucket and gave her a few gentle pats on the side and left.

I took my bucket to the milk cooler and poured it in. The cooler room was very clean. The cooler was a very large, stainless steel tank with a number of hatches on the top of it. These hatches were where you poured the milk in.

I was on to the next chore of the evening: giving the cows their feed. The older you got on the farm, the more responsibility you had—for a farm is a place where you work harder than anywhere else. It felt good once you were into the rhythm of farm life. I can say that because I did not have to live it full-time.

Getting up at five in the morning in the summer was an adventure for me, but I know it was not for my cousins because they had to live it every day. We got up early because the cows had to be milked. This was actually critical for the cows. If they were not milked, their bodies could be in a heap of trouble. This meant that there were no sick days, or holidays, or three-week vacations.

Because it was a change in my routine of life, I loved getting up early and watching that gorgeous, orange line appear on the horizon as you walked to the barn. The animals always seemed so joyous in the morning. The birds seemed to sing louder than any other time of the day. After doing the chores in the morning, we would all gather at the front of the cow barn and begin our walk to the house. I loved it because you could smell the homemade bread soaked in real butter and fried bacon coming out of the house. It was like a thick cloud to your senses. The actual sight of the table was even better than the smell had advertised it to be. There were eggs, bacon, a toast of white bread, homemade jellies, fried potatoes, honey, ham with brown sugar, and finally, real, whole milk right straight from the cow to the table. After we had eaten our fill, we sat there and discussed the morning antics in the barn—which were always funny.

After that, we discussed what had to be done in the afternoon. Actually, I just listened. Harold had to do some work with the tractor. That sounded pretty exciting so I went with him. When we got to the tractor, he just jumped up on it from the back and sat in the seat. There was only one seat, and it was metal. The fenders did not cover much of the huge tires, maybe covering just about four feet. He started the big, green machine, and we waited for it to warm up. I stood beside him as he set the throttle to a higher speed. This tractor did not have a cab or cover over the driver. We were both out in the breeze as we began to move. Harold drove us over to the area where the plows and rakes and discs were. He asked me if I wanted to drive, and I did—of course. I found out that you could get a workout driving this thing because there was no power steering. Once we got to the area where the equipment was parked, he took over. He asked me to get off because they were going to hook up the disc, and he said that you should not have someone riding when pulling the equipment. I jumped off the back of the tractor and watched as he backed that big machine up, as if he were an artist, and then hooked up the equipment.

It was now later in the afternoon. Ann, my cousin Carol, and I were just walking down the path to the barn in the four o'clock sunlight. The grass just seemed to be greener than normal, and you could see the rays of sun in the dust we kicked up from the pathway. "Follow me," Carol said suddenly as she took off running toward the barn. The barn then took on a dark maroon color because the side we were approaching was now in the shade. Carol ran around to the left side of the barn and to the door on that side. She opened the door, and we walked on the wooden floor planks. We walked across the planks to an area which had a cement floor. As we walked around the end of a wood plank wall, shafts of sunlight penetrated the gaps in the wood barn siding, and the light revealed all kinds of glistening, floating particles in the air. They seemed like shreds of silver floating in the golden sunlight. I swept my hand through them but could not feel a thing. The magic of the sunlight and the barn revealed even more things as we were all dancing around in what seemed like gold and silver raining down from heaven. Suddenly, Carol broke from the dance and ran about seven steps and screamed with joy as she jumped into a mountain of oats that was higher than her head. The oats were so deep I thought you could drown in them. "Watch this," she said to me as she worked her way out of the pile. She walked over to a ladder which was built into the wood wall of the barn. Ann and I followed her right up that ladder and onto a loft. Carol reached for a rope that was tied to one of the support posts of the barn. As she untied the rope from the post, my eye followed the long, sweeping arc of the rope to the other end. It was tied to a crossbeam, about twenty feet up. Carol stood on the edge of the loft, which was about nine feet off the barn floor where the oats were piled. Our eyes had to look like saucers. We both knew what was going to happen. Carol held that rope. She actually wrapped her arms and hands securely around it as she stepped off the loft. She swung out over the abyss on the end of that rope and let out a squeal of delight. As she reached the highest point of her swing, she went completely silent. Carol had our complete attention. Ann and I were hypnotized by the event. At that point, Carol let go of the rope. She hung in the air for just an instant and then dropped about fifteen feet into the pile of oats. There was no movement as her head and shoulders stuck out of the oats. The silence of the barn was broken by the loud yahoo she yelled as she swam her way out of that pile. I stood on the edge of the loft and grabbed the rope on its second return swing. I stood on the edge of that loft beam and gave a little push off. My sister gave an added shove as she said, "I want my turn." I swung out, and as I hit the highest point of the swing, a sound of joy erupted from my mouth as my stomach got that tickling feeling. It was time to let go of the rope. I was weightless for an instant. As I fell, my brain said, "I hope this does not hurt." The trip was about fifteen feet straight down into those silky, soft oats. I just could not get out of the oat pile fast enough. I wanted to do it again. Just as I stood up at the edge of the oat pile, a smaller body hit the center of the pile and let out a scream of joy. It was my sister Anne. We continued this for at least thirty minutes. Our hair was full of oats, and our sweaty bodies were coated with the oat dust. None of it mattered. It was such fun, and it smelled great.

We left the barn and headed for Aunt Isabel's house. As we were walking, we graded every swing we made. We entered the house, and Mom and Dad heard our conversation. Mom asked if we had been jumping in the oats. She interrupted our excitement. Mom and Dad then commanded us not to ever do that again. We looked at each other in shock. How could such a joyous thing be so harmful? Mom then explained. There could be a stick or branch down in that pile of oats, and we could be impaled on the stick by the force of the fall. Also, one of us could time our fall wrong and land on someone who was still in the oat pile. Dad and Mom were right. We never swam in the oats again. At least I did not.

One hot afternoon, I decided to go for a horseback ride. My cousin Harold had a horse named Major. I was always excited to see Harold. He was about four or five years older than me. I admired him greatly. I thought of him as a man of honor and great physical strength. I watched him work the farm, and I knew I wanted to be as strong as he was. He had complete command of Major. I thought I could too.

The hot August sun reminded me that the breeze created by a brisk ride on Major would be just wonderful. I had ridden Major many times, but this time, I was going to ride him bareback. They did it on TV all the time!

Major was grazing in the pasture under a blue sky, and he was a picture with his large brown and white blotches on his muscled body.

I walked across the pasture of green grass and jumped up on Major's bare back. His head snapped up to attention. He slowly turned to see who was disturbing such a fine, slow day of grazing the sweet-tasting green grass. He seemed to have a squint to his eyes as he glared back at the intrusion to his relaxing moment. I had not taken the time to put the reins and bit in his mouth because my plan was to pull on Major's long mien in order to steer him. After he had taken a long, hard look at me on his back, Major threw back his head. He did it so hard that it lifted his front hooves off the ground about two feet. I thought Silver reacted to the Lone Ranger in the same manner. This was not the same. I realized that after about five seconds. I realized that I was not in control of the monster whose back I was now captured on. Major had broken into a full gallop, and it did not matter how hard I pulled on his mien. He was on a mission. As he galloped, he consumed large amounts of air through heavy breathing. I too heard a slight rumble that almost seemed like a deep, audible giggle of joy. He was in control of the situation, and he was enjoying it. It sure did seem that way. I now could see that he was heading for the pond. The pond was about fifty yards in length with about fifty tall poplar trees around its perimeter. They were about twenty feet from the water's edge. The trees were spread about ten feet from each other. I thought that Major was thirsty, and he had decided to get a drink. That was when he started to veer toward a stand of maple trees which were outside the poplar trees' circumference. I was so busy staying on the back of this monster that I did not notice how fast we were approaching the maple trees. I looked up just in time to see Major duck his head as he ran under one of the maple tree branches. It was at the perfect height. It hit me right in the chest and swept me right off that horse's back. It was as if someone had swung a two-foot-thick baseball bat and hit me in the chest. The air was instantly pushed right out of my lungs. What little was left must have been knocked out when I hit the hard, dry ground. I blacked out for a few seconds because I remember taking a very deep breath and then opening my eyes. I saw a blue sky and a big tree branch above me. I wondered what had happened, and then, my brain started to function again.

Major had achieved his goal—getting me off his back. He was a big, smart, strong, and stubborn animal. As I gained more of my senses, I wanted to find a two by four and crack him across the head so he would know what it felt like. I sat up and turned my head towards the pond. There he stood proudly flicking his tail and sipping water from the pond. He was standing in about one foot of water. Suddenly, he lifted his head proudly and turned to look at me. I swear he was grinning.

That was my last ride on Major. They told me he died of old age a couple of years later.

Mom said that there was constant change on the farm. You never know what the next year will bring. You are never in complete control. Work like you are in control but remember that only God is in control—the farm would remind you of this every day.

LOAFERS ON THE FARM

The fashion of the day, month, or year was of little importance to me until I was about sixteen years of age. It seemed like there was a switch on the side of my head and someone flipped it to a fashion-conscious position. White sox were suddenly very desirable no matter what else you were wearing. They also had to be the Adler brand. We would wear them with a sport coat, tie, and white shirt. If you really wanted to top it all off, you would wear penny loafers. You could actually put a penny in a special place on the shoe for all to see. This was considered the icing on the cake. I really desired a pair of those shoes very much. I began to save my money for the purchase of this fashion statement. I always took very good care of my things so Dad and Mom knew I was responsible. Mom said it was good stewardship. I did not know exactly what that meant at the time, but she said it was in the Bible, so I figured it was something good.

It was Friday, and Mom said that we were going to the shoe store in Hamburg—to buy a new pair of shoes. I was very excited. I was getting my penny loafers, and everyone would notice. I got home from school, and we all had supper. After that, we got into the car and headed off to the shoe store. We visited three stores and then headed back to the first store and made the purchase.

The days were becoming longer because it was spring, and the sun was still above the horizon shining brightly at eight o'clock in the evening. It was always exciting to have more hours of daylight. As we walked out of the store and into that sunlight, it seemed like God was honoring the purchase with His warmth shining down on us. The air was so clean and clear, and the cars all trumpeted their exhaust notes as they rumbled down the village main street of Hamburg. I had the shoes, and life was good. I was about to make my appearance at school on Monday, and I could not wait. We walked to the car which was parked on Main Street. Mom said that we were leaving for Grandma's house in Palmyra the next morning. I thought I couldn't wear my new loafers on the farm. Then, I knew we would be going to church, and I could wear them then.

That Saturday after we arrived, Uncle Clarence and his son Harold wanted to go look at a farm that they were considering buying. Dad said he would like to go along, and I said I would too. They would all be getting dressed up, and I could wear my new shoes. After a late lunch, we all got into Uncle Clarence's new, two-tone, blue Ford and rode over to the proposed farm. As we rode along, I noticed the pastures of dark emerald green. They looked as if they were giant carpets rolling over the hills. The angle of the sun was perfectly accenting the roll of the carpet on the gently sloping hills. The old trees seemed to say, "Look, notice our three-foot-wide tree trunks." It seemed like the trees were saying, "Can you see our wisdom?" It was like they were saying that they have seen it all as their big branches reached across the road to protect and shade it. We passed acres of fresh-planted crops, and then, there would be the electric wire fences separating the new fields from the perfect, green, rolling pastures.

Once in a while, we saw a wooded area and then a half mile of extremely black soil which contrasted with the bright, green plants that were freshly planted in it. The green seemed to glow in the pure spring sunshine. These dark, black acres were called muck farms. They were extremely fertile. Dad said that the soil ran like a river along the surface and could go ten foot under the ground. They were sort of like coal deposits. Sometimes, the muck could catch fire from lightning, and then, it would burn for days. I don't know how they would put it out.

We would drive for two or three minutes down a beautiful road and then turn to go down another. I did not know how long it took us to get there, but we finally arrived at the proposed farm. No one seemed to care about the farmhouse because we drove straight to the barn. Everyone got out of the car, and we walked right into the cow barn which had its doors wide open. The sunlight ran ahead of us straight into the barn. It caused the interior of the barn to glow brightly as the sunlight reflected off of the white walls. The golden straw glistened as it lied on the floor, covering the area where the cows would normally be. This barn was a very clean barn based on my standards. The cows must have loved it.

Dad, Uncle Clarence, and Harold were discussing various aspects of the barn as they walked slowly forward and deeper into the barn. We were walking across, and I lagged slightly behind as I was looking around. As I took a step, I stepped onto a small pile of golden straw. I knew I stepped wrongly because my foot quickly sank into a warm liquid hidden under the straw. I knew from the smell that I had stepped into the gutter where the cow urine was. My right foot was instantly saturated with the stuff. It did not matter how fast I pulled my foot out of that mess. My brand new loafer was filled with the urine instantly. I turned and removed my shoe and poured out the stinky liquid before anyone witnessed my stupidity.

I put my shoe back on my wet foot. My heart grew sick because I knew my shoe and sock were changed forever. My foot smelled badly. It was not a pleasant ride home, and it seemed to take so much longer. I did not talk to anyone on the way home because I was so irritated at myself for not paying attention in that barn. I was more concerned about the impression my appearance made.

I suddenly decided that no one paid any attention to what I was wearing. Dad and Mom had paid good money for these shoes, and I had wrecked them.

As the months went on, I polished those loafers every other week. I used the polish that Mom bought when we purchased the shoes. I would caress the right shoe with extra attention—hoping that I could delay what I knew was going to happen. The leather began to crack more and more with every passing week. That right shoe had been bathed in cow-manufactured acid. My polishing had delayed the action by about six months. The leather was just rotting away. The white sock left much sooner.

Mom said that we must have gotten a bad batch of leather in those shoes. I explained my stupid actions to her, and she began to laugh. She then asked me what I had learned. I told her that by taking my eyes and watching if others were watching me, I was not looking at what was really important. Taking care of what I have received is what's right. Mom said that that was actually an inexpensive education. Then she said, "What would you like to learn next? Just give me the money now." She laughed and held out her hand.

I guess you always pay for an education in one way or another. It's the cost of living. You can get a discount by listening and learning from someone else's mistakes. I needed to do more of that.

WHERE ARE YOU TAKING ME, DAD?

That night was one of the darkest my eyes have ever experienced in my fifteen years of life. The clouds were covering the moon and the stars. We were in a strange land. This only added to the anxiety of the moment. I noticed that all of the side roads were now dirt. There were no paved side roads for the last twenty minutes of our trip. We had already been driving for four hours. I knew we were heading north because the road signs I had seen said north on them. Even those signs were now rarer. I felt like we were leaving civilization. Dad, Teddy, Curly, and I were on a real adventure. Teddy was Dad's best friend, and he was telling me they had never been where we were going before. They had directions from some old guy who had died, and they never wrote them down. He just hoped that he remembered them correctly. Dad was driving, and Teddy would say that he thought Dad should turn at this corner or onto that road, and Dad would turn. The next thing I knew we were on dirt roads. It was not getting better. Dad said that we were out of paved road. Teddy asked Dad if he was sure of that. Dad just gave a shrug of his shoulders.

As we drove down that dirt road, I noticed that the trees were squeezing the road down. The darkness was also increasing. We came to a fork in the road, and Dad slowed to a stop. Then, as he turned the wheels to the left, he said, "Let's try the left fork."

I looked out the windshield just in time to see the road disappear from view. In the next instant, the front of the car dropped down and reconnected with the road at about a thirty-degree angle. When we had reached the bottom of the hill, my eyes were drawn to the left side of the car. I could just barely make out a pile of logs that looked to be fifty years old. I also saw a faded sign on the side of a weathered building. It said McFarland's Marina and Supply. It all looked like it was older than the log pile. I asked myself if people lived here long ago. I was concerned. I had to remind myself that I was with Dad and his friends. I would use that thought to calm down more than once.

Tension was through my body. I could tell because I had to tell my muscles to relax. I knew we were in a foreign land, and even though I was with Dad, I was still concerned. Dad's friends had told me that if they caught you fishing illegally in this country, they took all your belongings and threw you in jail. I guess that fear was there even though we were not doing anything wrong. That was when Dad broke my thought pattern when he said, "Hang on." The headlights were shining straight out into the darkness. There was nothing in front of us. Had the earth dropped away from the car? The headlights slowly started to descend downward. When the lights hit the road, we were on our way down the steepest hill I had ever been on in a car. It must have been at a sixty-degree angle. As we were nearing the bottom, I could feel Dad trying to apply the brakes. The hill was so steep that the tires were sliding on the dirt road. Everyone else in the car was smiling but me. I guess they thought they were on a thrill ride or something. Dad finally nursed the car to a stop at the bottom of the hill. We slowly started to roll forward again and approached a very narrow dirt road on the left. He turned down the road and drove about seventy-five yards.

The lights of the car turned quickly to the right. They hit a redwood-stained house which actually looked new. We pulled right up against the building and stopped. Teddy and Curly got out of the car and walked around the corner of the house and out of sight. Dad left the headlights on because the darkness was so heavy. Dad opened his door and got out of the car and stood and stretched in the cold night air. I immediately opened my back car door and stepped out behind Dad. That was when the house lights came on and the outdoor spotlights came on. Dad walked around the corner of the house with me right behind him. I saw a carport with the entrance to the house about halfway into the carport.

Dad entered the house, and I followed him. Once we were in the house, I saw the lights were bulbs in light sockets nailed on to exposed two by four studs. The interior of the house was completely empty of interior walls or paneling. There was framing for the bathroom and shower stall. Paneling was on the outside of the bathroom walls. There was also framing for the kitchen cabinets. That was when Dad told me that he and his friends had formed the R-Ten Club which had purchased this property. There were seven members in the club. They were in the process of completing the interior of the house. Dad handed me a bucket and a flashlight. He told me to go across the road that led to the house. On the other side was some tall brush. Go through that brush and on the other side was a fast-flowing creek. I needed to fill the bucket with water and bring it back to the house. As I walked away, he told me to watch out for bears. I stopped dead in my tracks and turned. Teddy then added that all I had to do was make a lot of noise and shine the flashlight all over.

I walked out the door and began praying for protection in a very loud voice. I shined the flashlight all over the place as I approached the brush on the other side of the road. I pushed through the brush, and there was crystal clear water flowing just as Dad said. I carried the bucket of water back to the house. Dad met me in the carport and opened a storage closet door that revealed a water tank and an electric pump. He said that the water was needed to prime the pump so that it could fill the tank. That water was then used to take short showers, flush the toilet, and run the sink in the kitchen or bathroom. You could not do all of them at once, or the tank would be empty. Eventually, they were going to install a bigger tank and pump. Dad told me all of this while I stood and watched him prime the pump. I decided I needed to watch how it was done in case Dad was not there to do it. He explained each step and how the pump worked. He knew that I would understand the theory of operation. He then told me that the bears were very real, and no one was teasing about their presence. He reminded me to be really careful at night and make sure that no food was left outside—it would attract them.

It was the inner tension of your body that will tire you out faster than physical work. I was exhausted, and all I did was ride in the car.

We all sat on boxes, or buckets that were turned upside down around a kerosene space heater. It must have been about one o'clock at night. Dad, Teddy, and Curly were talking about what they wanted to accomplish this weekend when we were not fishing. Each person was getting their job assignment. It was very methodical and orderly. Each guy had different talents, so their assignments taped into their own talents. This meant that you got the best everyone had to offer. They finished up their session, and we finally went to bed. We slept in sleeping bags that night, and it was cold.

We were up at seven the next morning, and I was glad we had primed the pump to the water tank the night before. I also found out we had hot water. I realized that this was not to be taken for granted again. The cold air in the house meant that you had to move more to keep yourself warm. Teddy got the heater going while the rest of us prepared a tasty breakfast of bacon, eggs, fried potatoes, Canadian bacon, and sour dough toast coated with butter and strawberry jam. Everyone was contributing some kind of effort to the feast. That is how it works in a family. I made the toast. We set a door flat across two sawhorses, and we had our table. Paper plates made it easy to do the dishes after.

It was time to go fishing. I stepped out the door of the screened porch and saw the whole property for the first time in the light of day. The sun was extremely bright in the crisp air. That was a nice way of saying that it was still cold. I remembered that we were about two hundred miles north of our home—so it had to be colder.

Dad took a Johnson outboard motor out of a storage closet and carried it down to the water. He carried it down a path of dew-coated grass. The air was very calm and crystal clear as I looked all around. I was actually walking backwards looking at the house. I caught a glimpse of a smile on Dad's face. He enjoyed me enjoying where we were. The house was placed in a heavily wooded valley. To the right was the road I crossed for water the night before. Ten yards beyond the creek I fetched water from was a rock wall that ran up at about a sixty-degree angle. The surface of the rock was sparkling with some kind of mineral deposits as it collected the heat from the morning sun. I looked at the redwood-stained, contemporary style house set in a valley of pine and birch trees and woods rolling up a hill to the left of the house. It was quite a picture. I turned to see the dark water of the lake with the steam coming off of it. I noticed the path we were on was all sand now, and the rock wall continued out into the water and went below the water's surface about a hundred yards out from the end of the dock. As I stared at the beauty of the place, Teddy woke me up by saying that this bay was called Dent Bay on the maps of the area. I turned and saw two aluminum fishing boats tied to the right side of the dock. The sandy beach curled around to the right of the dock and led your eyes to the three houses along the shoreline which ran to the horizon in this thick fog. There was about fifty yards between the houses which were about three hundred yards from our place. As the fog lifted, I could see that same shoreline ran one mile out into the water.

Teddy and Dad mounted the motors on to the transoms of the boats. I got into the boat with Dad. Teddy and Curly were in the other boat. Teddy and Dad were working on getting the motors started, and Curly and I were loading the tackle boxes into our respective boats. The motors were started and warmed up. We started to slowly cruise out of Dent Bay and into bigger waters. The water appeared to be almost black in color. I asked Dad why it was like that. He said that glaciers formed this area long ago, and they carved out very deep bay areas of three hundred feet or more in some areas. I was used to the greenish brown of Chautauqua and the clear bluish green of Lake Erie. I asked Dad what we were fishing for. He said northern pike, which was a cousin of the musky. We had some hits on our lures that morning, but no fish were landed.

I listened very intently to the talk of these three friends. They were talking over the water from boat to boat. The water was very still. They would say what kind of lures they were using and whether or not they had any hits or follow-ups. They freely shared information when asked. Dad only answered when asked. It was obvious that these men trusted each other very much. I could see a loyalty here that did not exist with many men. Suddenly, Teddy cast his lure at our boat and right at me. It hit me in the right arm. I waited for the pain of the hooks as they entered my flesh— but it never came. I almost jumped out of the boat trying to avoid the incoming lure. All three of the men burst out into laughter as I observed that there were no hooks on the lure. I had been set up. I thought it was funny after. Dad said it was time for lunch. We all reeled in, and the motors were started for the run to Dent Bay. The air had warmed, and the coats and sweatshirts were now off. I was in the bow of the boat. I turned my back to the bow and lied back to enjoy the ride and sun and scenery.

We approached the dock and tied up the boats. Since there were no other people around, we left all of our equipment in our boats. We proceeded to walk up the sandy path to the house. The high, noon-day sun revealed huge carpets of dark green moss growing on the flat parts of the rock formation on our right. I wanted to explore. Dad said that I needed to be very observant and listen because of the rattlesnakes. I looked at him, and I knew that the word games had ended, and this was serious business. This place just had one surprise after another. I decided to go to the house with everyone else. It was time for lunch, and I was very hungry.

We had a great lunch, and now, it was time to work. Somehow, it just did not feel like work. Dad assigned me to do the lawn mowing. I had to cut the tall field grass in the front of the house with the rotary lawnmower. This would eventually become the front lawn. He and the others were doing some plumbing work and electrical work. Once I was done mowing, I went inside and received a new assignment. I had to cut some two by fours for wall studding. I watched how the wiring was done between my cuts. Everyone was contributing their talent to the completion of the interior of the lake house.

The goal was to have it complete enough so each man's family could come for a week or two in the summer.

I watched these men work, play, and even disagree. They never let their disagreements fester into anger. I was witnessing men who worked with true friendship, loyalty, and commitment. They had an even greater commitment to their families. They all had a very unique thing with each other. It was called a relationship. I never heard any of them ask "What's in it for me?" It always seemed to be "Let's do this." You always knew that the most important thing above all else was each man's family. This was the only thing above their friendship.

We all got together for dinner at about four in the afternoon. After dinner and clean up, we went fishing again. Dad caught a northern pike, and everyone got very excited. He caught another one about ten minutes later. The guys decided to name that spot Chick's Point. We would mark any maps we got with Chick's Point because he seemed to be the only one who caught fish there.

The darkness was starting to descend all around our boats, so we headed back in to Dent Bay. The air was becoming thicker and cooler. When we arrived at our dock, we emptied out the boats, dragged them up to the house, and turned them over. Once our outdoor work was done, we entered the house. The house was warm and toasty because Curly had gone in and started the heater while we were outside.

As we all sat around the heater, the men discussed what needed to be done on the property by the next work group. Dad wrote down the notes and placed them on the inside wall near the door with a tack. This became the procedure for each work group. The group coming next weekend would look at the note and know what had to be done. We were all tired from the great day, so it was time for bed.

The next day was Sunday. We were all up at dawn and had our cereal in paper bowels. Everything was cleaned up, and we were all packed up so we got into the car and headed home. The trip home in the light of day sure did have a different feeling. I knew where we were going and the quality of who I was with, and these made me feel better and deeper than when I arrived.

I now believe it was a miracle to be surrounded by these men, and I was smart enough to learn from them.

That was what my Father wanted all along.

Dig It

Summertime and the living were exciting. Games with any ball you could think of, water to swim in, biking, and of course, fishing. When I turned fourteen, I wanted to make more money than my paper route could supply me. I had goals of where I wanted to spend it already. I just wanted to move up the ladder as they say.

One day, I was throwing the football with my friend Doug. He was always working somewhere, and he never complained about it. He was the only one of my buddies who always had money in his pocket. Doug never flaunted it in front of us. He always offered to buy if someone could not pay for a popsicle, but he was not a welfare giver. He had to work hard for what he got to just give it all away. We took a break from the football and rode our bikes to the corner store. I started asking Doug what he was doing to make his money as we sat on our bikes with the kickstands down. We sat on our bikes and talked while we drank our soda pop. The sun glistened off of our clean, waxed, and washed bikes. Doug looked at me and, very seriously, said that he was digging graves at three different cemeteries. I did not laugh because this was a serious conversation. That was exactly why Doug just flat out told me what he was doing. He knew I was ambitious while many of our friends just wanted to play all the time. I was curious about how much he was paid for the job. I just asked him right out. He said that he was getting one hundred dollars for each grave. I did the math and realized that half of that in 1963 was very good money. My brain told me that it would take five weeks to make that money on my paper route. I asked him, "How long would it take for two of us to dig a grave?" He told me three to five hours, depending on the weather conditions and the ground conditions. Ten dollars an hour was a very good wage at that time. Actually, it was outstanding. I asked him if he could use a partner in his venture. He answered, "Sure I can." I asked him when his next job was. He told me where and when. We could ride our bikes to the job sites, and the groundskeepers would provide us with the tools of the trade. We would use shovels and picks. I was very excited to get started. I was not prepared for the education I was about to receive as a result of this occupation.

Tuesday came, and the day was warm and sunny. It was a very typical, summer August day. On this day, I was going to do a not so typical thing. I was about to dig someone's grave. The sound of that thought coming out of my mouth and across my lips was very different. It just felt different. I just kept reminding myself that the money was excellent, and someone has to do these kinds of things.

As we rode our bikes to the job site, the sun was becoming warmer. The birds were singing their joyous songs from the branches. Their song notes seemed to reach across the road to cover, protect, and bless us as we traveled. There was not a cloud in the sky as we turned to the right and passed through the gated entrance of the cemetery. I followed Doug as we rode to the caretaker's area. The caretaker took us to the site of the job and then informed us that the funeral would be at four o'clock that afternoon. It was about ten o'clock, so we knew we had to get to work. As he walked away, he turned and said that he would pay us another fifty dollars for covering the grave after everyone had left. He knew we would stick around.

The digging itself was very hard work, but it was summer, and the ground was still a little soft from the earlier rain. This was helpful for digging. The sun was high in the sky and very hot on our backs, but we both kept our shovels moving. It was as if we were shoveling the money. We both stopped to rest for only a few minutes. I looked at Doug, and he looked at me, and we both agreed. This was a real person's grave, and we were excited to be digging their grave. Somehow, that could not be the correct way to think about it. Our conversation was then shifted to how we should really think about what we were doing. We both decided that we were performing a good deed that the family would never really think about. We settled it in our minds.

We finished digging at about two thirty in the afternoon. We rolled out the grass mats. These covered the freshly piled soil to form a nicely finished area for the people to stand on. The people would not really see the evidence of our work. We even made sure that the grass carpets were draped down inside the grave so that the people could not see the dirt on the sides of the grave. No dirt was left exposed. We took our shovels and picks and went about forty yards away behind a stand of trees. The afternoon shade, by now, was greatly appreciated. We were out of any line of sight of the funeral procession.

The people began to arrive at the site. The process took quite a bit of time, as people were moving slowly toward the burial site. I guess they were trying to delay the inevitable. The sorrow could be heard and seen. We could see them, but they could not see us. We were not trying to be nosey, but I wanted to learn what to expect and how to respond to such situation. Dad and Mom always said that we should try to learn something from every experience we have, whether it was good or bad.

The lowering of the casket was just beginning when one of the ladies began wailing in a sound I never heard before. It was the sound of ultimate pain. The thing that struck me was that there was no way to offer any help. I realized that the Comforter was their only help. I hoped that they leaned on Him.

This whole experience caused Doug and me to have a very powerful discussion about what we were witnessing. We both agreed that our bodies were nothing more than rental units. We turned them in for new ones when this unit was worn out. We agreed that our mutual belief in a heaven was a comforting factor in our lives. We decided that the graves we were digging were actually for the living. Life had a process, and this was a part of the process. There was comfort in knowing that there was a beginning and an end.

This leaded to a new life, and a much better one in heaven. What was in those graves no longer held any life and was of no use other than being a fertilizer. This greatly changed my outlook on cemeteries. Their purpose was for the living to see memorials, but nothing is actually there.

With this discovery, I learned to respect the monuments as memories, but I had no fear of walking through a cemetery at night. In fact, many of our friends thought we were crazy to walk through a cemetery at night, or even in the daytime.

One time, we convinced our friends into a cemetery to show them a grave we had dug for a funeral two days away. They were afraid to even look into the empty hole in the ground in the middle of the day. These were some of the same people who had made fun of us. Doug and I decided to have some fun with our hecklers. I bet two of these guys five dollars each that they could not walk through the cemetery at night. I was surprised that they both took the bait. On an agreed upon night, they would walk through the cemetery.

I made sure that we had dug a fresh grave on the agreed date. Of course, they had no knowledge of this. They also demanded that I go with them and show my bravery too. They walked right into our perfect plan. The night of the event came, and it was perfect. It was a little breezy and cloudy, but an opening in the clouds would appear just often enough to cause dark shadows. The trees were being moved around just enough to cause the shadows to come to life. We entered the cemetery, and you could see the hecklers eyes become very big. Their breathing matched their eyes. They were taking very deep breaths while their eyes were opening wider. They made me promise not to run ahead of them. I had no problem making that promise as I guided them on my planned path. The clouds were covering the moon as if on purpose. I was leading these two right by the hole we had dug earlier that day. The trees actually were creating a sort of moon shade right over the hole. The area was completely dark and seemed even darker because of the brightness of the moon around it.

The air was full of the sounds of the trees rustling and the branches hitting each other. Sometimes, you would hear the squeaking sound of two branches rubbing against each other. It was even better than we could have planned. Doug was standing in the hole but right next to the edge where we were about to pass by. He had worn dark clothing, but I could see him. There was just too much tickling of the hecklers' senses for them to concentrate. They were a nervous mess, this quiet duo. As we approached the hole, I mentioned that we were about to walk by a grave that Doug and I had dig that day. The branches seemed to scream out at that very moment. The two big mouths looked up and at that very moment, Doug was able to grab one ankle of each of them. At the same time he said in a very deep voice, "Who are you?" The explosion occurred immediately. The screams were extremely loud, and they raced past us extremely fast. I knew that their big mouths were opened for the last time as far as their trash talk about us was concerned. We could hear their bodies smack a monument as they were running out of the cemetery. Doug climbed out of the hole and said that they were downright unsociable. We both broke into a good belly laugh together.

The next day, I was riding my bike by the corner store and saw these same two boys standing there. I just rode slowly by and said, "It's your money or your life." I never expected to see the ten dollars from them, and we never mentioned it again. They kept their mouths shut from then on. They never understood why we did the job we did. We did it for the money.

We would dig two graves a month in the summer and far less in the winter because the ground was so hard. We should have done three or four a week in the summer and saved it all. I could have paid cash for my first new car and paid half of my first house with the money earned in just two summers.

We learned some great lessons about work. People knew we were not afraid to work. More important was the witnessing of how people respond to very severe stress. I was more appreciative of my parents, grandparents, and family because I still had them with me. I knew that we all have our time to go. I learned that we should not fear it but do more for others while we can. Doug also helped guide me down a new path with our many conversations on faith. His excitement over Billy Graham and his life and goals caused me to dig for more truth. Thanks Doug!

THE ARRIVAL

I thought that most young boys who were the firstborn of their families wanted to have a brother to pal around with. Some of us even went so far as to pray for a brother, and I did—for a number of years. Then I became a teenager, and other things cluttered my thoughts.

I was grateful to have two wonderful sisters. We always had fun together, and we had some very funny situations. I was greatly blessed to have them in my life.

I just decided to pray for a brother again when I hit fifteen. I guess I just got out of the habit of praying for a while.

The answer came when I was sixteen years of age. I was so excited when we learned that Mom was going to have an addition to the family. We had no idea if the baby was a girl or boy. We all learned of his arrival on March 23, 1962. Anne, Becky, and I were at home when Mom brought the new arrival in the front door of our little home. We knew that this was a miracle—as all children are. Mom made sure that we all held the little guy right away. We were no strangers to babies because someone was always having one somewhere in the family. Mom said that his name is John Chester. I was impressed because that was Dad's name reversed. He had Dad's name. What an honor!

I would hold, feed, and even change John's diapers. This was not a once-in-a-while event. It was a pleasure that I was able to do it very often. The diapers were of the cloth variety, so you had to know how to fold and hold them. Of course, they had to be cleaned and washed. This was just part of being a brother. At least that was what I thought. I also learned how to apply the talcum powder and do the safety pins. This was actually preparation for my own children many years later. How was I to know? Mom and Dad were always passing on knowledge without telling us they were doing so. My sisters and I all took our turns at babysitting John. Mom had three very willing helpers on this new project. We would all help in the cleaning and washing of the bottles. This all had to be done before the bottles were sterilized in boiling water. It was an ongoing task which we sometimes grew tired of—then we remembered whom it was for. The great thing was that we all never grew tired at once. It was a rotational thing. I guess that was pretty normal.

It was not very long before John was walking all around the house. If we had a fire burning in the fireplace, we knew he was heading straight for it. We would grab him and pull him away. It actually became a game. We would all be laughing as we pulled his giggling body across the circular rug by his little legs. We never jerked him around. It was always done in a loving way. His curiosity always peaked whenever I had to put a fresh log on the fire. I would let him come and stand right next to me and be very close to the fire. He could really feel the heat with the screen pulled away and the hearth wide open. He blinked his eyes in the heat and brightness and stepped back a little. I know he figured out that this fire could turn out to be a bad thing. You could see he was really thinking about what was happening. His desire to get close seemed to be quenched.

John had always been a very determined person when his mind was made up. Like most children, he would get upset if he did not have his own way. In fact, he was getting more and more worked up as the days went on. He would hold his breath in anger. The length of his breath holding was getting longer. I was wondering what was going on, and Mom did not have an answer right then.

One afternoon, he went through his routine and held his breath. Mom picked him up from the floor when she saw that he was turning blue. As she held him, he would not inhale fresh air.

That was when I saw his little arms go limp. I dropped to my knees and cried out to God to save my brother as I wept. My face was down on the floor. I lifted my head to see through the tears that Mom was holding John's head under the cold-water faucet while she shielded his face and mouth from the running water. I heard John take a very deep breath as his little body lurched when he came to. She immediately pulled him from the water and held him close. I got up from the floor and hugged Mom and him— and not a word was said. After a few moments, Mom said she was taking him to the doctor.

Later, we learned that Mom had taken vitamins during her pregnancy, and of course, those passed on to John. The problem was that he got too much of some vitamin. It was all cleared up. We had an answer to the problem and a solution. John stopped holding his breath as his system balanced out.

I believe that God, Mom, and the doctor all had a role in this being taken care of. It all worked out right. John was normal except for his tremendous curiosity.

Christmas was on its way, and we were all very excited to see how the new arrival would react to it. He loved the lights and all the decorations and joy we felt at this time of year. He was one of us!

The colors and the brightness were just so stimulating for his mind. You could see it whirling in his head. *What is this electricity thing?* He did not say it, but you could see he was trying to figure it out. He would look at the wall socket and then look at the lights. I thought he was a very bright little boy.

I set up a small train track layout on the black tile floor. He was very fascinated. I saw him look at the wall socket where the transformer was plugged in. The lights were plugged in and now the train. The connection for him was that this was the source of the power or something. The temptation to do research was just too great. One day, I saw him hanging around the wall socket that I had the train plugged into. It just happened in a twinkling of an eye. John had taken a fork, and he stuck it into the wall socket. He screamed just as I knocked him off of the handle of the fork. I was amazed at the speed with which this all took place. His hand was burned in the thumb area. Mom picked him up and put some butter on the burn and ran cold water on his little hand. He was a fast healer like the rest of us. I think we must have inherited that trait from Dad. I also believe he was protected again. I also believe the same thing for my own children today.

The following summer, we were all excited that John would be having his first adventure at the R-Ten cabin in Parry Sound, Ontario. My friend Tom came with us too.

Once we arrived at the R-Ten house, we staked out our bedrooms. They were small bedrooms, but each bedroom had two sets of bunk beds. They were handmade from solid oak boards. They were each held together by sixteen three-quarter-inch-thick bolts made from solid brass. The wood had a very light stain that accented the grain of the wood beautifully. The sets were extremely solid and heavy. This meant that you could jump around on them, and they would not flex or move. They were so solid that they did not even make any noise. The R-Ten men did excellent work. This quietness was very important when you were getting up early to go fishing. You would not want to wake others in the house. The unpacking was done, and we were up early the next morning to go fishing with Dad. Dad caught a small northern pike, but he threw it back. We returned to the cabin where Mom had already started a big breakfast. Tom and I jumped in and helped with the toast and fried potatoes. Anne and Becky set the table. It was about ten in the morning. After breakfast, we were all relaxing while reading books and playing cards or board games. It got to be one o'clock, so we decided to try some water skiing. We skied behind the fishing boat. Dad was the driver, and he loved to challenge the skier. He would do figure eights with the boat and take you back over your own wake. You would be laughing and working to stay up all the time. Dad was laughing too. It served to make us better skiers. We all went back to the house and relived the experience with our stories to Mom. Dad would be smiling and laughing as we told what he did to each of us. We had a late lunch of sandwiches. It was time for a nap before dinner and fishing that evening.

John decided to stroll into our bedroom with his flashlight even though it was daytime. A flashlight was always a great toy for a two-year-old boy. We threw a light blanket over him as he walked into the room. I grabbed his little shoulders and spun him around twice. He giggled and laughed as he walked out of the room wobbling from side to side under the blanket. We pulled the blanket back into the room, and he came in again with a big grin on his face. We did the same thing again, and he let out a squeal of glee from under the blanket. I know we repeated this at least six times with the same result. Tom and I marveled at his determination. Finally, he entered the room and crawled up on my bed exhausted from our games. We took our nap together.

That evening we went fishing with Dad. John and Mom waved from the dock as we left. He wanted to come with us, but he did not cry about it. His fishing time was coming.

The next morning, we got up to go fishing, and a heavy fog was upon the surface of the water. It was extremely dense. This was not something to go out on the water in. We all went back into the house and into our warm beds.

We got up again at about nine that same morning and walked down to the water to observe the fog situation. It was starting to be burned off by the warm morning sun shining down from the cloudless sky above.

The water level that year was very low. You could actually stand on dry sand right next to the end of the dock. The dock was completely out of the water. The deck of the dock was at shoulder height when you stood on the sand next to it.

There was a slight breeze from right to left as you looked out over the water from the dock. I noticed it when I walked up the path to the house to meet John as he was walking toward us. He took my hand as we walked to the dock together. I explained to him that he needed to stay up on the dock this morning. He walked out on the dock while I walked on the sand along the left side of the dock. He could see me walking downhill as the sand descended. Pretty soon, we were both at eye level with one another. As I got to the end of the dock, my eyes were at his knee level. He thought that was pretty cool.

Tom, Becky, Anne, and I were bending down and picking up flat stones. We were seeing who could get the most skips out of a stone. Dad was standing to the right of John up on the dock. Dad was quietly observing our contest. I bent down to pick up a nice flat stone. I stood up and looked out at the water. It looked like a piece of glass. The sun burst out of the fog and a warm mist came across my face from the right side. I was about to enjoy the moment when a certain odor entered my nostrils. It was very familiar. I opened my eyes and turned my head to the right. I looked through a rainbow of color and saw the source of the mist. John had decided to relieve himself off the end of the dock. Dad burst out in a belly laugh as I lurched for cover from this urine acid rain. He had told John to go ahead after John asked for permission to go. I got out of the mist while the others roared in approval. John just finished his duty. I took a shower after we all made our way back to the house.

When I went in the car or for a walk, I would always take him with me. It was great to see him checking new things out. You could tell that his brain was always in gear.

John grew up very healthy. In fact, he still plays hockey to this very day. He loves his own family very much as we were all taught to do. His curiosity led him to eventually be an executive with IBM.

I observed his preparation for his purpose in life, but that is his own story. We all as brother and sisters admire his accomplishments. The Father prepares each of us in His own way.

My First Blister

High School is a world all in its own. There were no taxes, or bills like car payments, or a mortgage to pay. Your cares were really very few. Your friends, music, girls, and sports were your cares as a freshman and sophomore. Yes, there were also your grades. We really did think that the subjects taken were most important. It was actually thought that the grade you received went along with how much you learned. What a concept.

I admired both those who got good grades and those who did well in sports. Those who did both, I thought, were exceptional.

As I reached my junior year, I actually was attending the school dances on a consistent basis. I did not have a date or one girl friend. I was inspecting the stock. That was what we would tell someone who asked what we were watching.

Tom, Lance, Dave, Ron, Clint, and I would take our morning walk through the halls—sometimes, as a group and sometimes, in pairs. It depended on when our buses would arrive at the school.

One such morning, I noticed this cute, blond girl who was always happy and smiling. She had real, platinum, blond hair and very fair skin. I noticed who her girlfriends were, and I knew some of them. I saw Linda at the next dance we had, so I asked her to dance. I was surprised to find out she knew my name. It was only a matter of time, and I was walking her through the hall on the morning patrol. I walked with her about twice a week because my friends were acting as if I had disowned them. They really let me know it too. I finally asked her to a dance. She accepted, and I told her what time we would pick her up. I asked Dad if he would do the honors of driving me to the dance and making a pick up on the way. I was not driving yet, and I really did not see a great need to be. Dad was grinning when he asked for the times of the pick-up and retrieval. I told him the times. That was when he said, "So you have a blister now, have you?" I knew a blister was a sore a person got on your hand from working on something for a period of time. Whenever you did something, the pain of the blister would remind you it was there. It was a small infection that would go away if you just let it rest. It really made me think about it. He said those blisters never let you forget about them. They either boil up or go away. I was really thinking about what Dad meant. That was a good thing, because then, I was not thinking about the blister, I mean girl.

As far as Dad was concerned, all of my dates were blisters.

When Dad would pick up my date after any dance, he would just nod and say hi. No other words were ever spoken by him. He would take us to my date's house where I would get out of the car and walk her to the door of her house. Usually, the mother would open the door and greet us, and I would just say good night. I turned and walked briskly to the car, and Dad and I would talk football or something on the way home.

I asked Linda to go to a house party with me, and she agreed after I told her whose house it was, and that the parents would be at the home. Dad asked whom we were picking up as we got into the car to go. I told him it was Linda. He said, "You know a blister can turn into an infection, and you asked this blister out twice." I knew exactly what he was getting at.

We picked Linda up, and she sat between Dad and I in the front seat of the car. We did not talk until we got out of the car. I told Dad what time to pick us up, and he nodded and left. Linda and I walked about ten steps down the snow-covered path to the front door. I knocked on the front door, and we entered the house. I would never do this normally, but there was a lot of laughter and talking going on in the house. I knew that they never heard us knocking on the door. Bonnie met us at the door and apologized for not answering our knock. We were at Bonnie's house, and I greeted Bonnie's mother. I had been her paperboy, and I knew her family from church.

I helped Linda take her coat off, and we proceeded to enjoy the friends and the conversation. We had soda pop and chips and snacks and Christmas music to set the mood. Bonnie's mom made sure that everything was all right, and then, she said she would be in the kitchen if we needed anything. Our favorite records were playing as we were all talking about things that happened at school that Friday. I sat down in a chair, and Linda decided to sit down on my left leg but not across my lap. I really did not think anything of it. As time went on, my leg began to fall asleep. I decided to move Linda to the side. I had two sisters, and sometimes, this same thing would happen. I was kinder to Linda. I put my hands on Linda's hips to move her just slightly. At that moment, she jumped up whirled around and slapped me in the face. I was amazed and surprised because I had no idea what I had done wrong. There was no talking with Linda after that. Dad could not have arrived early enough to take us home. I was angry but not embarrassed because I did not think I did anything wrong. We did not talk in the car. When I got out of the car to walk her to the door, I made sure I kept out of slapping distance. When Linda reached her door, I said good-bye and turned and walked back to the car. When I got back to the car and got in, Dad just gave a *hmmm* sound. As he put the car in gear, he said, "I guess that blister is healed." He was right.

I was usually meeting girls at the dances, and once in a while, I would take a blister to a movie or house party. Dad would often have a comment when we had dropped the girl off, and we were in the car alone on our way home. They were quick observations he would make. He made me think.

One Saturday, Dad only had to drive half a mile to pick up the girl with the long, brown hair. I went to the door of the house, and she opened it and came out into the breeze. That hair moved in such a soft motion across her face and then, swept back in a wave-like motion. She entered the car and said hi to Dad. He actually talked to her. Dad's conversations were very short. This was a first. We had a great time at the dance, and Dad was outside the school waiting for us. This girl had no problem sliding into the car and out of the cold. The color of her hair matched the leather trim on her furry coat. She just said, "It is really cold." Dad said, "Yep." He then gave a nod of his head. That was a big deal. She just did not know it.

We arrived at the dance and had a wonderful time. The dance ended, and Dad was there to pick us up. We rode home, and all were very quiet. As she slid out the door of the car, she said bye to Dad, and he nodded and said bye too. I walked her to her door and said goodnight. I got back into the car for a short ride home. Dad asked, "What is her name again?" I said, "Janice." And Dad nodded like always. He never called her a blister. He must have known that this girl was already an infection. Infections can spread through your body. If you give them enough time, they can enter your heart. That's why you must be careful. Time was on her side.

I think that was the last time Dad drove me on a date. My friends were driving now.

I did not want this feeling in my heart to subside. I would not let go of it. It was like nothing else was important. Even my friends were second to her. I wanted her to be "the friend."

The first blister had come and gone, and I was healed of her and many others. This girl was very different in every way. We dated very often, and I saw no need to continue the selection process. I think Dad knew it. Mom always wanted the selection to continue. That's what moms do.

Dad was a good reader of his son's heart. I hope I inherited that trait.

Classy Men Who Sang for Their Supper

"Come on we are going to practice," he said. Then I asked him, "Practice for what?" He just asked me to follow him. Tom was a great friend, and I trusted him as we made a left turn off the main hall of our high school. He opened a door which led to a narrow hallway. We entered the hallway and proceeded down to it. The hallway was kind of dark, and the grayish green walls gave it an eerie kind of feeling. The air was musty because there was little ventilation. Suddenly, Tom stopped in front of a door on the right side of the hall. The door had a ten-inch square window right at eye level, and light beamed out into the hallway from it. It actually produced the only light for the hallway. Tom opened the door slowly. I wondered why he was being so careful. I followed him through the doorway and into a room which was brightly lit. Clint, John, Bob C. and Urs were already in the small room. John was seated at an upright piano. Clint was deciding what was going to be sung next as Tom and I entered the room. I had no idea that such rooms existed in our school.

The room was heavily soundproofed. Once you were inside, it seemed like the rest of the world no longer existed. You could really concentrate without any distractions when you were in a practice room. I asked how many rooms like this were in this area of the school. Bob C. told me there were six practice rooms.

He said that was pretty good for a school of our size. Normally, such rooms were used for private lessons on instruments. Bob C. found out which rooms were not in use, so that we could use them to practice singing.

I felt so joyful as we began to sing together. I could pick out some parts of the harmony for myself, and the blend of the voices in the room was like a rainbow of colors. The voices seemed to flow like paint canvas. Like colors of paint complimenting each other, our voices seemed to flow the same way. It was as if someone had planned for all of our voices to come together at this very moment. I thought that I could do this every day. It was a magnificent experience and surprise.

These guys were all friends of mine. We had played football and baseball and attended basketball games together. We even patrolled the school halls in the morning together. I think some of them were shocked that I could sing. They were even more stunned to hear me sing in harmony and not be affected by the other singers. I asked when they would be doing this again. The answer was that they would be doing this twice a week. They were actually in the process of forming a band. I was surprised to hear of this, but I knew immediately that this was something I wanted to do.

Urs was a foreign exchange student from Switzerland, and he would be going home upon graduation at the end of the school year. If he intended to stay in the band until then, there was not a spot for me. I practiced with them anyhow, and things worked out because Urs did have to go home. He left the band after a few weeks. I had my place as I had hoped.

The band had decided that the proper dress for performing would be that all members should be dressed the same. This was actually decided before I was a member. The members informed me that I needed to purchase a burgundy sweater, white shirt, and black dress pants. I thought that their choice of dress was superb. As the weather grew warmer, the dress changed. The weather was growing much warmer, and we all loved the sound of The Beach Boys and their beautiful harmonies. We also liked their yellow- and white-striped shirts and white pants. That became our summer attire.

Bob C. and Clint were the real musicians of the group. They both could play other instruments. Bob C was a lineman on the varsity football team. We already knew each other and had a mutual respect for one another. He was a tremendous trumpet player. He knew how to read music and had a sense for what people liked to hear. He could also play the trombone and tinkered with the drums. He could also sing bass and had an ear for what voice parts sounded good. We all loved to watch Bob C. at the dances because he knew how to talk to the girls. He was the group master in that area. He was always respectful, and the girls were always attracted to him—his good looks and good posture.

John played the piano and really was prepared to execute whatever Bob C. or Clint had in mind. John was always dressed very well and made sure that the rest of us maintained a clean, presentable look. He was not afraid to tell any one of us what needed to be done. His head nodding in approval of an arrangement was always a good thing.

Tom had a very good singing voice. He had a great ear for picking out harmony parts by simply listening. He could also read music, and he could play the harmonica, which was a unique and good thing to have in a band. He had the lead on songs like "Go Away Little Girl" but he sang back up most of the time.

I was just a backup singer. I could read music a little because I had played the clarinet for two years. That was an advantage. As time went on, I actually got to sing lead on a couple of songs. I loved singing "More." I was always singing it to Janice whether she was there or not.

Clint was a magnificent singer, and we all knew that he would explode on the national scene at some time. In fact, we all wanted to see him have success because he was a really good person, and he had a God-given talent. He could sound exactly like Johnny Mathis.

Actually, Clint had his own style which magnified his great stage presence. When he was on stage, all eyes were on him. He literally took command of the stage. He had a great range in his voice and very good breath control. He always established a relationship with the audience. He could tell them stories and laugh at himself, and the next thing you knew, they were hanging on his every word. We were just like the rest of the audience. We loved to see him work. He always gave his all during a performance, and the sweat that rolled off of him was a proof.

We worked in the practice room on some backup singing for some songs that Clint had written. It was really wonderful to be part of a much bigger picture. When we sang some backup harmonies for Clint, the picture of sound seemed to fit so well. I thought that the songs were really good. They songs were "I Won't Cry" and "I'm Warning You!" Bob C., Tom, and I would sing backup harmony while John was on the piano, Bob on guitar, and Rick on the drums. Sometimes, Clint would play trombone and Bob C. would play his trumpet. They were both very good musicians. Clint could play everything. He was just amazing.

I wanted to sing better, so I started to take voice lessons from Clint's mom. She was a classy lady. You always wanted to be proper when you were around her. You just sensed her elegance without her even speaking. When she walked into the room, she stood very straight. Her hand movements were graceful, and her steps seemed as if she was sweeping into the room. Sometimes, when she spoke, she would emphasize her words to make sure they were clearly understood. I thought that she just had a presence about her. This might be because she was an opera singer in England when she met Clint's dad. They met when the US Army stationed him in England. Sometimes, Clint's dad would be at the house when I arrived for a voice lesson. He was always in a good mood. He was a very friendly man with a great sense of humor. He exuded kindness without ever saying it. You knew he was a generous man. It was obvious that he was a real gentleman. I believe any parent would want their children around people like them. I think I was blessed to know them. They allowed us to have many practice sessions in their home, which was not a big place to have such a noisy event taking place.

The band became known as The Classmen. Actually, the name of the group was decided long before I was a member. I did think that it was a very cool name for the group.

The Classmen performed at many high school dances and community events. I think we played at a wedding or two and some fire,halls. Then it happened.

Clint was a songwriter from the start, and we performed his songs with him in the lead while we sang backup in all appearances. He explained to us that we were to record his songs at a studio which was owned by a local radio personality. He informed us of the date, and we all became very excited. We also got the chance to work on our harmonies. This was the build-up to the recording session at the studio in the city. We actually practiced a lot of our singing parts at Clint's house. As we finally got to the day of the recording session, there was an air of excitement and apprehension all at the same time. We arrived at the studio, and I was disappointed. It just looked like a plain old house from the outside. I had seen too many movies that glorified the Hollywood version of a recording studio. Those didn't exist in real life. We started to unload our equipment from the two cars and take it into the studio. Now, you could see that this was a recording studio. We took the drums to one area of a large and open room. There were microphones in key areas and small, sound-absorbing walls in various spots. One area was for the lead singer. Another area was for the drums and another for the backup singers. We stood in our area with the wall to our back, and the microphone suspended on a boom in front of us. We each had our own cubicle, but we were all in this large room. The room was thirty feet wide and forty feet long. It was brightly lit and had a ten-foot ceiling. There was a sound-deadening tile on the walls and, of course, on the ceiling. There was a room with a ten-foot-long, five-foot-high window overlooking the whole area we were in. Inside that room was where the sound technician had the soundboard and controls for all the microphones and recording devices. There was a loud speaker for him to talk to us on. The first words to come out over the speaker were, "Step it up boys, 'cause you are now on the clock." The studio was rented by the hour, and we were now paying. This was the first time I felt any pressure. I knew we had to get this right, and it had to be done quickly—this actually added to our excitement. You had the feeling that you were now entering something big. It was time to take a deep breath. I noticed some of the other guys doing the same thing. Clint must have noticed it too because he called us all together and said, "Calm down, and let's all take a deep breath together." He said, "Relax." Then he had a big grin and said, "Let's do this right."

We all went back to our designated areas. There was time for a short warm up, and the sign came from the sound booth that it was time. We kind of snuggled up to the microphone and did our thing. It was almost too good to be true until we heard the playback of the recording. It was not up to our standards. In fact, it was disappointing. The backup singers were out of key, and it was very clear to the ears. Whenever you hear yourself on a recording, it does not sound the way you think you sound. The recording did not lie. We had to adjust very quickly. We must have made five recordings of each of the two songs. When they were played back, we picked what we thought was the best one. We all thought that Clint did a great job on all of them, but we came up short as backups. Our harmonies were still flat. Money was talking louder and louder as our session came to an end. Our time had run out, so we picked the best recordings of the two songs.

About two weeks later, we each received some demo records. The idea was to play them for people like a preview. People thought that they sounded pretty good. Each time I played a record, I could hear the flaws. We learned that we had done what so many just dream of. Clint's dad reminded us of that very fact. It took a while to realize that he was right.

About two weeks later, the real records arrived at Clint's house in boxes, and it was very exciting to see them. Some people bought them when they were at our performances, and a couple of radio stations actually played our songs on the air.

We continued to perform for some community centers and youth centers. We just had a good time together, and it was fun meeting different people.

One Saturday night, we were heading home after a performance. We decided to stop at a local restaurant because we were all very hungry. It was about one o'clock in the morning. I guess we were just being typical eighteen-year-old boys with bottomless bellies.

We stopped at a Your Host restaurant. They were open twenty-four hours, so it fit our requirements. We walked in the front door and headed straight to the back of the place. All of these particular restaurants were laid out the same way, so we knew exactly where to go.

The eyes of the few patrons were all over us. This was pretty normal because you seldom saw six or seven guys with matching clothes and clean, short haircuts walking into a restaurant at this hour. The eyes of the employees were upon us also. I think it was the sweaters and white shirts that threw them off, or maybe, it was the politeness that we presented.

We had the back of the restaurant all to ourselves. We grabbed two tables and slid them together as the waitress observed us. She thanked us for doing her work. We were just thankful to have a clean restaurant to go to. The waitress asked what we were doing out on this rather cool fall night. The answer was that we were a band called The Classmen, and we had just finished performing. She had that puzzled look on her face as she looked silently around the table. We were all nodding yes. She could not help but challenge us to sing something. We looked at each other and started to sing "The Way You Look Tonight" and "Go Away Little Girl." The waitresses were never offended. They were usually flattered, and then, they smile. The few patrons that were there went silent and just listened. Sometimes, Clint would really get into it, and the next thing we knew, the patrons had left their seats and come to the back of the restaurant to stand and listen. When we were done, they would all clap their hands and smiled their approval.

The waitress would be beaming a smile as she asked us what we wanted to order. We enjoyed our food and beverage. The waitress came over and talked as we were eating, and she would ask how often we performed. When we were done, we would move together and sing "Good Night Sweetheart," but it's time to go. She would blush and smile, and then, the other employees would make a quick move to hear what we were doing next. It was always a joyful experience for the restaurant and us. That was exactly how we wanted it to be. The restaurant showed their appreciation by not giving us a bill. That happened quite often, and we greatly appreciated their act of kindness and hospitality. We never entered expecting this to happen, so when it occurred, we knew it was special.

Each of us was getting older, and our lives were starting to take us in different directions—as life does. The performing jobs for the group slowed down, and eventually, The Classmen band was gone. No one actually said we were disbanding or anything, it just evolved as our lives do. The truly, wonderful thing was that the memories kept playing on.

Bob Carlson the trumpet master and singer settled in Minnesota and then moved to Iowa. He has received many national awards as a marching band director. His bands have marched in the Rose Bowl and New York City Christmas parades and many others. He is considered to be one of the best marching band directors in the nation. We still get together about twice a year.

John Wolfrum the piano player became a science teacher.

Tom Dusenbury was in management with a chain store company and is now a successful health insurance executive.

I became an industrial arts/technology teacher, a businessman, and now an author.

Clint Holmes has gone on to have a hit record in "Playground in My Mind." He has earned Emmy Awards for his TV shows. He was entertainer of the year in Las Vegas for a number of years and had a theater named after him. He is now working on a Broadway play—which he has written and arranged.

I have great joy thinking about our times together in high school and with The Classmen. I feel very blessed to have been around people who want to achieve. Their attitudes affect you all your life. That is what has been passed amongst us without knowing it. The great thing is that we have embraced and accepted it. Whenever we get together, we all know that life has even more great things in store for us. We have a special bond that few people get to have. We are friends to this very day.

HER MOTHER MADE HER DO IT

Springtime is when the tree sap flows freely. The birds seem to be happy and free to fly north. It just seems that life is free to move on. The sun rises earlier each morning and sets later each day. It was as if it had fewer limits placed on it. The relationships developed over the confined winter months just seem to blossom in the spring. The number of dates increased, and the girls glowed more than ever. The whole world is expanding right before your own eyes when you are seventeen. Every day is a whole new experience.

I was dating Janice, and my best friend Tom was dating Cheryl. I could look at Janice forever. Cheryl was a cheerleader and a fun person. Whenever the four of us were together, we were laughing and having a wonderful time together.

It was track and baseball season. Tom was an excellent hitter on the baseball team, and I was a sprinter and jumper on the track team. We both enjoyed sports and any outdoor activities.

As the days grew longer, it felt wonderful and odd to go to a dance at seven in the evening while the sun was still out. Our brains were telling us, *the sun is out, why are you going indoors?*

After the school dances, it was magnificent to walk out of the building and feel the warmth of the evening and Janice's hand in my hand. Why did it seem like it would always be this way? Our lives revolved around each moment. The moment changed when Tom started to drive to school. His dad bought a 1955 light blue

Pontiac. Sometimes, Tom would drive it to school, and I would ride with him. The body of that car was pretty solid for a ten-year-old car. It had just a hint of rust on its very thick steel body. We decided that it would last a lot longer if it had a new paint job. The longer sunny days would provide us with plenty of time to do the job. We had never done anything like this before.

We masked off the chrome with masking tape and added two racing stripes on the hood. We made two wide stripes of masking tape on the hood, so that when we removed the tape, the original, light blue paint would show through. Tom got some dark blue paint from somewhere, and we went to work.

The sun was shining through the maple and pine trees on its way up to the driveway where we were working. We stood looking at the car. Tom had the brushes in one hand and the can of dark blue paint in the other hand. He opened the can, and we began to paint the old warhorse with our brushes. You have read that correctly! We were painting a car with brushes. We did not miss a spot, and we made sure that we put it on nice and thick for the following winter months. We were thinking ahead. We also discussed the brush marks that were left. We thought that, perhaps, the paint would flow together and smooth out as it dried. It did not. We both stared at our finished work. Neither of us could help ourselves as we broke out into hearty laughter. Tom's dad came out to inspect our work. He was a big man. He slowly walked towards the car while puffing on his pipe at every other step. As he got close, he pulled the pipe from his mouth and softly said, "What the." He then leaned back and grinned. He turned towards the house and chuckled, and he shook his head as he walked back into the house. As he entered the house, he pronounced that the car certainly should not rust next winter. We could not wait for the paint to dry so that we could see our craftsmanship, but we did.

Tom drove the car to school the following Monday. During the school day, our buddies would ask him if we painted the car with a brush. When he answered yes, they were speechless. It gave everyone something to talk about for the whole week. It was usually someone who did not have a car to drive. I got tired of answering the same question, so I would fire back, "Do you have a car to drive to school?" Their answer was always no. So I would tell them that this brush-painted car was better than theirs. Some got the message.

The car always made the visits to the gas station an adventure. We would ask for fifty cents worth of gas, and the attendant would be distracted and ask if those were brush marks in the paint. Sometimes, we got an extra gallon for free because of the distraction. All the stations knew the car eventually. We had left our mark.

The car did not rust the following winter just as Tom's father had stated. We rode it to the choir practice every week that winter. It was a tank in the snow, and we loved it. If we had ever hit anything with it, the object would have been destroyed. The car would have been untouched. That was how we felt about it. We never had an accident, so the theory was never tested.

Tom and I were both taking post-graduate courses at the high school. We had both graduated with New York State Regents diplomas. We were told that we would have a better shot at college with the extra courses, but I did not think it mattered. A side benefit was that we both could be with our girlfriends. That one year just seemed to drag on because you could not take part in any activities. Spring was coming. Truthfully, that one year gave us time to mature a little more and face the coming challenges a little better.

Spring came, and school was done. It was time to take another step into life. We both got summer jobs at the Water Authority with the help of my Dad and Mr. Vukelic.

Our family would spend many of the sunny Sundays together at my Grandma Malinowski's. We usually had a barbeque outside. We all loved eating outside. You never had to worry about the mess you might cause on the floor. We had just finished our early dinner at about four in the afternoon. Tom suddenly rounded the corner of Grandma's house and said hello to everyone in the backyard. He had never just dropped over like this before, so I knew something was up. He asked if I could walk out to the front yard with him. We walked across the green grass and under the branches of a black walnut tree. The sun was warm, and the rays fell down through the pine trees. We walked along the cars parked in the driveway towards the road, and it suddenly caught my eye. It was tan with a matching color interior. It was a Dodge Polara convertible. I was amazed. Tom's father had bought it the day before. Tom told me to get in. When my rear end hit the seat, Tom started the engine. We both just grinned from ear to ear as we sat there listening to the big V8 rumble through its nostrils, as if it was talking to us. How can something sound so wonderful and be so powerful. It almost seemed to be alive. This was my first time in a car with no roof. As we backed out of the driveway, I looked straight up at the blue sky squeezing between the branches and pine needles of the two fifty-year-old pine trees on either side of the driveway. Their trunks were about two feet in diameter, so one was always careful backing out of this driveway. We were lined up straight on the street after backing out, so Tom gave the gas pedal a light tap, and the beast lurched forward. Wow! He hit it again, but he did not put it to the floor. He did not have to because the point was made in the lurch. As the breeze in our hair began to build, we both were smiling as we turned and looked at each other. The smiles were screaming of approval without us making a sound—the wind in your hair, the sun shining in all its glory, and the trees seeming to raise their arms to hail our passing, like a dream.

We would have a similar experience many more times that summer. It always felt good every time. We were blessed, and we were thankful.

One Saturday, we decided to take Janice and Cheryl on a date. We learned one lesson real quick. When the girls were in the convertible, you had to have the top up. The girls did not want their hair messed up by the breeze. Sometimes, they would just let us have it their way. Tom picked up Janice and I first, and we all rode to Cheryl's house. When Cheryl's mom saw that the car had bucket seats, she demanded Cheryl to take a pillow so Cheryl could sit closer to Tom on the consul between the seats. Cheryl said that she could not do that, but her mom insisted and handed her the pillow. Cheryl got into the car and explained why she had the pillow.

We knew that we were going to have a wonderful time together as we rode to our favorite ice cream stand. The ice cream place was right on the shore of the lake, and we all loved looking at the sunsets. We finished eating our ice cream and got back into the car. I asked Tom about the submarine races on the lake, and he went to a beautiful spot and parked. We could look right out the windshield of the car and see the sky picking up the pinks and the purples of a gorgeous sunset. It was amazing to see the sun had slowly set. Once the rim of that orange ball touches the horizon, it was almost as if the hand of God grabbed it and in a few minutes, pulls the sun out of sight. The sun disappeared below the water without a ripple or a sizzle. A purple line along the horizon took its place.

Janice and I sat in the back seat hugging and kissing. Cheryl put that pillow up on to the consul as instructed and sat up on it. She and Tom were kissing. Janice and I were watching the lake and them when I saw just a wisp of smoke coming up from Cheryl's seat and pillow. I told Janice that she must really be heated up. Just then, another wisp appeared. I could not help but say wow. I could not believe my eyes. What did he have that I did not? Cheryl answered the question I never asked out loud. Cheryl turned and slid off of the consul and grabbed the pillow.

She said the pillow was getting very warm. I said, "Duse, you are something else." Duse was his nickname. Now, the smoke was apparent to all in the car. Cheryl picked up the pillow. She held it up, and we could all see the smoke coming from a hole that was burning in the center of the pillow. All of our mouths assumed the shape of an O at the same time. Then we all broke into laughter as all our heads turned to Cheryl in amazement. How could this be?

When Cheryl threw the pillow onto the consul of the car, she did not notice that she put it on top of the cigarette lighter. When she sat on the pillow, she pushed the lighter in causing it to heat up to its maximum temperature. She was fortunate enough that the pillow did not burst into flames. We now knew she was really one hot babe. Tom took the pillow out of the car and put some lake water on it to make sure the embers were out.

It was wonderful describing this to our parents because her mother made her do it. Our parents shook their heads, and we had lifelong memories to live with. We are still together and have gone back to that very spot many times in the last forty years. The fire of our friendship has never gone out. I could go for some ice cream right now.

THE BLACK MARIAH

At sixteen or seventeen, most boys are involved in cars, and that is the topic of most conversations. The girls were a topic of conversation also, but they were not the main topic when they were not around. Cars were the main subject. I would listen and learn because I had a lot of ground to make up. I did not become interested until I was a junior in high school. The guys would be talking about this new car called a GTO and how fast it was. Dad was a mechanic, so he really knew cars—but in a very different way from my friends. He was always thinking reliability and how easy they were to fix. He told me that high performance meant high maintenance.

I did not have any interest until Tom was telling me about this Ferrari. I had no idea what a Ferrari was. He showed me a picture, and I was in love. Then, I told him I had never heard of Ferrari. He was astounded that I did not know. He told me that they were probably the best fast cars in the world. I knew I needed to do some research on these cars, or I would be left in the dust.

I started to pay attention and read car magazines and listen to the gearheads. I started asking Dad some questions. I knew that Dad was surprised at my interest because I had not shown any before. He had rebuilt many engines. He knew it all—literally. After I had turned eighteen, he asked me what kind of car I liked. I answered, that for some reason, I preferred Fords. Then I went a step further and told him I wanted a convertible. He did not think that was a good idea because of all the extra things that break. I knew I wanted one after I rode in the Dodge convertible. Dad told Mom that I had the fever for a convertible but maybe it would go away—it did not. Dad was not partial to convertibles because they had too many moving parts, but he said he would look into it.

We had a discussion on my income and the costs of operating a car. He already knew what my income was because he was the one handing me the check each week. Dad just wanted to make sure that I knew.

I drove over to the Ford dealer one Friday evening and looked at the used cars. I was always going dreaming. That did not mean that I was not buying right then. I was just finding out what the market place had for me. I was also educating myself on the prices and how much bargaining room I had. I really could not tell a good car from a bad car. Dad could.

One day, Dad came home from work and said he had talked to Jim, one of the salesmen at West Herr Ford. Jim told Dad that a man was buying a brand new car from him. He was an organ and piano tuner, and he kept his cars meticulously. Jim said the car the man was trading in was a 1960 Ford Sunliner. Dad said it would be the right car for me. I did not even hesitate to doubt or question Dad. I knew that Dad knew cars, and he really knew me. That meant that it was a done deal. He explained to me that the car was taken care of very well. He told me that he had looked at the car that day. It was a black convertible, and it would take some care to keep it as nice as it was. He said that I would learn good maintenance skills with this car. He told me we would go to the dealership and sign the papers and pick it up on Saturday. I did not know what a Sunliner looked like, but I would know soon. This all happened on a Monday evening.

Finally, Saturday came, and Dad and I went to the dealership and talked with Jim. We signed the papers, and I had my first car payment. It was nerve-wracking and exciting at the same time.

Everyone we met at the dealership, Dad called by his or her first names. Jim said congratulations to me and told me to follow him so we can put the plates on the car. He handed me the keys, and we walked out the front door of the dealership on Clark Street. We turned to the right and walked along the front of the building. The sun reflecting off of the large plate glass windows of the showroom felt so warm and comforting. We came to the end of the windows and turned to the right. That was the first time I saw it. It was parked along the side of the building. The wide chrome grille was glistening in the sun. The chrome strips took your eye to a long, flat hood. Dad told me it was black, and it sure was. It had a black convertible roof and a tinted glass windshield. The closer I approached, the more I could see the contrasting interior of red, white, and black. That red was a lipstick red. The outside edges of the seats had black and white stripes. The front seat was a bench-style seat. It had an automatic transmission and a 352 cubic inch engine. The chrome trim was pitless and, the interior was immaculate. Dad was right. This car was beautiful.

We, actually Dad, drove the car home and pulled in the driveway with a big smile. He parked alongside his station wagon. He drove it first to make sure that everything was correct mechanically. When he got out of the car, he went straight to his garage and came out with a can of car wax. He handed me the wax and said that this car will only look great if it was constantly waxed. I started waxing my car right then. I finished up the waxing and put the top down for the first time. I took the boot out of the trunk and snapped it down over the top which was folded down in its compartment behind the backseat. What a wonderful feeling of freedom to be in the driver's seat—with just the blue sky and God for your cover. The chrome that was all around the windshield had glistened in the sun. I turned the key, and the V8 rumbled as it awakened to my call. This was not a performance car, but it was a powerful car. Today, it would be called a land yacht. The car just seemed to glide down the road. As I approached the end of my street, the giant, old maple trees seemed to cover the entire road. Their arms were covered in a green velvet robe of leaves that draped over the branches to provide cooling shadows. The shadows and rays of sun that shot down through the leaves had a great visual effect of dancing all over the freshly waxed black paint. It was like diamonds were jumping out of the paint.

The June breeze went through my hair and over my skin as I cruised under those wise old trees, and it brought great joy into my heart and mind. I just whispered, "This is what we were made for." The only thing I needed was Janice's hair moving around in the breeze of the car.

The Old Lakeshore Road was a complete joy to the senses. As I drove, I could feel the temperature changes and the smell of the freshwater and blossoms along the road. I did not get the same effect with the top up.

The gas attendant told me that it was a nice car as I asked for two dollars' worth of gas.

Dad had guided me to the right car, and I had agreed with him. It was Sunday, and Dad said he was taking the car to work the next day. I just said ok. Monday came, and Dad came home from work. I found he had filled the tank. He enjoyed the car and would take it to work twice a week or more. It just all seemed so right. When Dad and Mom went to a wedding in Rochester, we all rode in the Black Mariah, and Dad drove it. He named the car. He knew she was reliable. He picked her. He wanted a big, safe, and reliable car for my first car. That was exactly what we got.

Since that first car, I have purchased eighteen new or used cars from that dealership. I know now that number nineteen will be black with a red interior.

Dad always said, "What goes around comes around." The older I get, the wiser he becomes.

THE BOSS IS BOSS

It was a beautiful July day with the smell of field flowers drifting into our yard from the fifty-acre field behind our house. The white clouds were slowly sliding across a powdered blue sky as I looked up from the blanket Mom had spread out across the emerald green grass of our backyard. The birds flew across the yard and then circled back and landed on the lawn and picked the grass for bugs and worms. My six-year-old mind was whirling with questions: *How do the birds fly? Why do robins eat worms and bugs and cardinals eat seeds?* There must be reasons for all of these things. I can eat almost all edible things, but I cannot fly. All of these thoughts filled my head while I ate my peanut butter sandwich and watched my little sister Anne. I made a decision that I guess it was all right that I could not fly.

Mom interrupted my thoughts with the statement that it was four thirty. She said we have to fold up the blanket. We have to pick up Dad from work. I asked what Dad did for work. Mom said that he was a mechanic. I asked her what a mechanic does. She told me that he fixes things—mostly cars, but he can also fix machines and trucks. I said that Dad must be very smart. Mom said that he was as we were getting into the car. My sister Anne and I sat in the backseat. It was my job to make sure she sat up straight and did not move around. There were no seat belts or child seats. When we got to Dad's plant, Dad would get into the driver's seat. Mom would just slide over to the passenger's side.

Our home was about a half hour from Dad's workplace. Mom pulled into a parking area in front of some overhead doors which were open. She was parked far enough away from the two doors to allow traffic in and out of the doors. She explained to us that, normally, the beer trucks go into those garages, and some men would reload them for the next day's deliveries to the stores. Dad would fix them when they were broken.

At that moment, a man came walking out of the darkness of the open doors and into the sunlight of the day. He was walking toward our car. The man had graying hair and was just less than six foot tall. He smiled as he approached our car. He said to Mom, "Hi!" He asked Mom who were the good-looking children in the backseat. Mom introduced us by name to Mr. Vukelic, and he shook my hand and said he was glad to see us. He also waved to Anne as she sat in her place on the other side of the car. Mom and Mr. Vukelic talked for a few minutes, and then, he told her that Chick was just cleaning up and would be out shortly. Chick was Dad's nickname. As Mr. Vukelic turned to walk away, I opened my hand and saw something green folded over about four times. I unfolded it and saw it was a dollar bill. In 1952, a dollar was worth a lot. I told Mom and showed her the bill. She told us that Mr. Vukelic was my father's boss, and he also owned the company. As she talked, she got tears in her eyes. She told us that he was a very kind and generous man. She then stated that I needed to save that dollar. I gave it to her because I did not think my pockets were deep enough to keep it from falling out. She took the dollar and put it in her purse.

When Dad came out of the doors and got into the car, Mom showed him the dollar and explained what had occurred. Dad just looked at it and nodded twice. He never said a word. That was a *wow* expression for Dad. Over the next five or six years, every time I would ride with Mom to get Dad—which was just about ten times a year—Mr. Vukelic would come out of the building and discreetly give me a dollar—every time! As Anne got older, he would give her one too.

I thought that bosses were very kind men, but Mom said that Mr. Vukelic was not your normal business owner and boss.

In 1958, I was twelve years old. I remember Dad was doing a lot of thinking for about a day or two. Dad was not one who sits around contemplating things. He was always doing something. I found out later that Dad had an opportunity to work at the local Ford Plant for, considerably, more money an hour. Mom said he decided to stay at Try-It because Mr. Vukelic had been loyal to him. He also thought that the company would really grow. Dad said that loyalty was something money could not buy, and you are only as good as your word. He had given his word to Mr. Vukelic.

Over the next few years, Dad would take me fishing with the Vukelics. I caught my first large-mouth bass with them in a boat on Lake Erie. Mr. Vukelic's son Gene said that it was the largest bass he had seen in a while. I made the catch about a quarter mile out from their family home. It was their encouragement that helped me get excited about fishing, along with Dad, of course.

If anything ever broke at the Vukelics' home, they would call Dad to fix it. He was always paid, and sometimes, he took me along. One of those times was when the walk-in cooler in their basement broke. Dad took me along, and I got to see how beautiful a family room could be. It had bleached pine walls everywhere and was completely carpeted. I was having my own dream session. No one else I knew had such a place in the '50s.

One Saturday, I rode to the plant on South Park with my Dad. I was a tenth grader, and I was proudly wearing my varsity football jacket. We entered the garage area where Dad's desk was, and Gene was standing in the ray of sunshine as it beamed into the opened garage area. He stood straight up and said, "That is a beautiful varsity jacket, and I bet you are very proud of it." I said, "Yes sir, thank you." He did not have to say that, but he knew what it meant to me. He was a fine athlete at college and knew the feeling. Dad was proud of it too. I saw Gene glance at him and smile. Dad just gave two nods of his head. No words were exchanged. They did not need to be. These two men knew each other and each other's ways. Dad's friend Teddy was there also. Teddy was a supervisor at the Bethlehem Steel Plant. The three of them were very good friends. In fact, Gene and Teddy were Dad's best friends. Actually, I was witnessing three dreamers coming together and making their dreams a reality with their friendship and trust in each other. The three of them formed a club along with some other friends. They called it the R-Ten Club. There were never ten members. I guess that sounded right. Dad really enjoyed fishing for northern pikes and was really concentrating his efforts on that particular fish. Gene, Teddy, and the others also had the same infection, so they purchased a house about three hours north of Toronto on the Georgian Bay to pursue their goal. That goal was to catch northern pikes.

Our family had been going to Chautauqua Lake for the past eight years. This was a change I was not totally in favor of. As time went on, it became more and more of an adventure every time we went for a week or two. Each member of the club would get a week or more for their family. I believed that Dad, Gene, and Teddy were the backbone and leaders of their club. They always seemed to be organizing and leading some new venture for the club. I watched the loyalty between the three of them and the friendship. They could disagree on things but were never disagreeable with each other. It just seemed that anytime I was around them, they would be joking and laughing with and about each other. It was a wonder to see Dad enjoying life and his friends. We would go to his place of work on Saturday just to be with his friends. I was just tagging along because I wanted to be with Dad. I saw and learned so much more.

Dad was right. The company expanded greatly under Gene's leadership. Dad wound up running the truck fleet of about fifty or more trucks. He knew he was a part of something that was much bigger than any one individual, and he loved being a part of it. My brother John and I both worked part-time for the company. Then John worked full-time for a while. We both pursued other careers just because we wanted to.

The company has now moved into its fifth facility. Gene has built the company to great heights and planned a celebration dinner. He made sure that Mom was invited. He also included Dad's name and involvement in the company's success. That's loyalty and friendship coming back after many years.

Dad passed on in 1988 after about three years of being in and out of the hospital and hardly working because of illness. The company still had him on the payroll. He never did get to really enjoy any kind of retirement. Dad enjoyed Christmas and New Years with the family so much that I think he willed himself to live through the holidays of 1987.

Mom needed a car, so Gene let her keep Dad's company car. A few years later, she needed a newer car. Gene gave her a salesmen's car from the company for ten percent of the car's real value. He told her that the company would maintain and service the car. They did up to to this day.

I know that I have been blessed to see loyalty and integrity in action. I saw it in my Dad first, and then, in those he surrounded himself with. They are all examples to me.

I want to accomplish the same and not break the chain of honor!

A Ride to Eternity

It was 1965, and the auto industry could do no wrong. My self-education and study of cars had created a person who was very excited about whatever Detroit was going to do next. Anything they made was selling, and it seemed like the companies could not make a mistake.

I was at Matty's barbershop waiting my turn for a haircut. The main topic of conversation was the new Ford Mustang. Just this one car seemed to create a frenzy of interest in all cars. It had everyone's attention and mine. The barber had a postcard with a picture of a Mustang convertible. He had it taped to the mirror that you faced when you had your haircut. I left the barbershop with a fresh haircut and a fresh desire for an exciting car. I was driving Dad's car home thinking about that Mustang all the way.

A few weeks later, Dad and Mom were doing some shopping, and they decided to go to a brand new shopping plaza called South Shore Plaza. The sun was glistening in the powder blue sky as we turned into the plaza parking lot. There were not many cars in the lot yet. I think that many people did not know that this new plaza was open. As you looked off in the distance, you could see one of the Great Lakes, Lake Erie, catching the glints of the sun on its surface and sending it back to our eyes. The white-brick buildings of the plaza set against this backdrop made you glad to be alive.

Then my searching eye caught the vision of a dream brought to real life. She was just standing there, not moving, dressed in white, and looking absolutely beautiful. I know my mouth must have dropped open. I was definitely staring, and I knew that was not polite. Dad rolled past her and did not seem to notice her. He found a parking spot near the stores that they wanted to go to and parked the car. I looked back and could still see her. She was standing there all alone. I knew I had to make my move to see her. All the rest of the family got out of the car and walked excitedly toward all the new stores. I followed until we hit the sidewalk. I told Mom I would meet up with them later. I turned and headed for the vision I had seen. She was still there, and I was amazed. I just wanted to get close to her and really check her out. She was clothed in glistening white that seemed to glow like a pearl. The white looked whiter because of the perfect accent of the blue stripes running right up her center. She had special mag wheels and redline tires. She also had real racing mirrors, dual exhaust, and a hood scoop that really functioned. I made sure that I never actually touched her as I looked inside through the door glass. There was no backseat. This was no ordinary Mustang. It was a 1965 Shelby Mustang. I was smitten. I walked away slowly and looked at her as I backed toward the plaza. I turned to walk back to the sidewalk, but I could not take my eyes off of her.

This man walked up to her smiling and unlocked her door and got in. He put down the side glass immediately. He started the car, and you could see him grinning from a great distance. The car just sat there shaking the ground around it. He would hit the throttle and rev it for an instant to warm it up. It was like a lion that would warn you with a couple of roars before it actually pounced. The driver carefully engaged the clutch and the car began to move. You could sense that he was trying to hold it back with chains, but it really wanted to leap forward. The car rumbled out of sight, and I let out a sigh. Dad walked up to me and said that I had the fever really bad. I just watched Mr. Shelby's sculpture disappear from sight.

Now, we were all touring the new plaza. The plaza could now close as far as I was concerned because I saw what I wanted to see, and I was done shopping.

Many weeks later, Dad asked me what kind of car I would like other than a Shelby. I told him that a Ford Falcon Sprint would be nice. He said that it would be too small for a first car. He managed to get me into the Black Mariah, but that was another story. He would always tell me about a car on a Saturday or Sunday. Then he would say that we would have to wait a week to talk to the dealer a second time about it. He always told me to calm down and that the car will still be there. He was right every time. He wanted to make sure the dealer did not steal my emotions. We were always dealing with the same dealer and the same salesman. Dad's approach was emotionless. He had a kind of "take it or leave it" approach. He said that you will never run out of cars, but the dealer can lose us as a customer.

Two weeks later, I was driving by the dealership and was looking at used cars in their lot. I had owned the Black Mariah for a year. I was not even thinking about having another car at this time. When I drove by, I saw a 1964 Falcon. I turned into the used car area and got out and walked over to look at the Falcon. It was powder blue with a dark blue interior. It also had a four speed on the floor and a V8 engine. It was also a convertible. I was off the wall excited when I got home. I had asked our salesman Jim how much they were asking. He told me, "Fifteen hundred dollars." When I arrived home, I was doing the math in my head and knew I could afford it. I told Dad, and he said that he would talk to Jim at the end of the week. "But…" I said. Then Dad blurted out, "The car will still be there." He reminded me that we wouldn't want to lose our advantage. Time will work for us if we let it.

Friday came, and Dad said that I was to meet him at West Herr that afternoon. I met him there, and he saw the car. Jim gave him the keys and walked away. Dad started the car and let it warm up. Then he just turned it off. He opened the hood and looked around and shook his head. I thought that something was wrong. When I asked what was wrong, he just said that I have a good car now. I told him that this was the one I really wanted. I asked him if we were taking it for a drive. He said that we did not need to. We walked back inside to Jim's office, and Dad said thanks to Jim, and we left. When we met up again at home, Dad told me that the car was good, and we just need to wait until the following Friday. This time, I only opened my mouth to speak, and as he walked away, he said, "The car would still be there." I thought that someone would buy it for sure. I actually stayed away from the dealership because I did not want to be disappointed. It was a good thing because I did not show any more interest as far as they were concerned.

Dad reminded me that I wanted the car, but I did not need it. I needed to get control of the wanting part.

The following Friday, Dad and I went to the dealership and closed the deal with Jim. We did not pick the car up until Monday. This time, I drove the car home. I thought I was in a really hot car. When I got home, Dad just reminded me that tires and brakes cost money to replace. He also told me that this car did not have as much mass around me to protect me. I needed to drive more carefully. He knew how a young man could get carried away behind the wheel of a car with a little power. This car was lighter and faster than the Black Mariah. It was also more controllable when used correctly. This meant it would handle in the snow with control. I took the car to an empty parking lot which was covered with snow and ice. I found out what the car would do—handling wise. Because of the snow and ice, I could learn this at a much lower rate of speed than normal. I thought that this was much safer than finding out the hard way on the street. Dad thought that was a pretty smart way to find out, but he reminded me that this was not a racecar.

Dad took the car to work twice a week, and I thought that was pretty normal. Our family had the use of two cars, and it just seemed right to me. Dad enjoyed the car as much as I did. I think that he even came home once with the top down. He told me that this car was very well-balanced.

I tested the quickness of my Falcon against some Chevys—which had larger engines. I was impressed because nine out of ten times, we came out on top.

Dad heard me bragging and reminded me that all of the companies have cars that were assembled very well, and that some cars were not. I just happened to have one that was assembled well. Mom said I needed to be grateful for this and not brag. It was my blessing, and I had little to do with it.

Mom had a friend named Flo. Flo had married Jim a year or two before. Jim worked at the local Ford stamping plant as a supervisor. Mom was friendly with Flo, and because of this, I was introduced to her husband. We really hit it off, and I found Jim easy to talk with. We would always get into conversations about life and how to handle certain situations. It never seemed to be light and meaningless talk when we were together.

One evening, we were at a party or function, and Jim needed their new S-55 Mercury convertible driven home. Jim asked if I could do that for him. I was humbled, honored, and surprised all at the same time. The car was beautiful, expensive, and only a few weeks old. The fact that he trusted me with this machine made a big impression. I was extremely careful and drove it straight to Jim and Flo's house.

One gorgeous spring day, I drove over to Jim's house with my Falcon. He was outside washing his car under the bright morning sun. I pulled my car over to the side of the road and walked over to him. I asked if he would like to take my Falcon for a fun drive. He said that he would receive great pleasure from that. His questions and answers always made me think. He said that was his purpose. He walked over to the car and slid behind the wheel.

I was in the passenger seat, and I was paying close attention to what he was doing. I knew this would not be a typical drive because Jim was not typical. He fired up the engine and engaged first gear carefully. He went through the four gears as we approached the first corner. He then downshifted as we went around the corner with a right-hand turn. He was smooth and deliberate. It was like his conversations with me. His motions had purpose, and it was like every move was thought out in advance. We came to the next corner, and we started into a controlled slide, and when he got on the gas again, he was in the perfect gear to accelerate. I was watching a concert. That was what it seemed like. I could see that Jim was headed for Route 20. Once we were on Route 20, he ran up through the gears, and we were cruising smoothly at sixty miles an hour. He turned to me and said that the car was well-balanced. Dad told me that too. He explained that the Mustang used many of the same parts and frame. I thought that was a pretty neat piece of information. I loved information, and Jim knew this from our many talks. He turned and looked me straight in the eyes, and then, he asked if I had ever read the Bible. I answered, "Yes." Then he asked me if I believed in Jesus Christ as my savoir. "Yes," I answered without hesitation. I was not expecting to have this conversation, so I was sure that I looked surprised. That did not slow Jim down one bit. He then explained how it was written in the Bible—that Israel was likened to a fig tree in the Bible. I told him I did not know that. Then he said that when the fig tree blossoms, His coming is near. Something inside me jumped, and I was amazed that I understood what he meant. It meant that when Israel blossomed, Jesus was coming soon. He then told me to look it up when I got home. Jim just smiled as we pulled up in front of his house. When he got out of the car, he said "Now, that was a ride for eternity."

I pulled away from Jim's house and went into thought about what had happened. I drove home and went up to my room. I proceeded to look up what Jim had said about the fig tree. It was all in the Bible exactly as he said it was.

I was reminded of all of the Sunday school teaching and my faith in general. Seeds planted long ago in a young boy's fertile mind. He had poured water on the seeds, and it was ready to come to life.

In one short ride, Jim had reminded me of what was really important. He brought me back to what life's real purpose is.

That was certainly going to be a very eventful twenty-first year on this earth.

THE MAN ON THE MOON

S pring was underway, and Janice was working for a dentist, and I was working at least two or three part-time jobs. We were newlyweds, and we just did what had to be done. I had two more years of college to go, but I thought life was good. I loved Janice so much, but I just did not tell her enough. We were both adjusting to each other. Marriage is a very gradual process.

We were riding down Delaware Avenue to pick up our first brand new car. It was a 1969 Mustang Mach 1. I was really excited to start shifting that four-speed and listening to the dual exhaust sing in its deep voice. We signed the papers and walked out of the office and into the showroom. We turned to the right, and there it was, facing us with its eagle-like front end. I must have stood there in shock for a moment. I stared at the green gold paint glistening in the perfect lights of the showroom. The flat black hood and the locking hood pins kept my eyes on hold. It felt like we were in a dream when Janice and I opened our doors and looked inside our car. Janice and I got into the car, and in unison, we took a deep breath as though it had been rehearsed. We just sat there and visually took in all that was new. The plates were on, and the salesman said that we were good to go. He reminded me that it was easy to spin the tires in the building. I must have had that look, and he had seen that look before.

I engaged reverse, and we carefully backed out of the building. The sound that resonated off the walls of the inside of the building was glorious. I put the shifter into first gear as Janice said, "Be careful." We were now on the side street which led to Delaware Avenue. It was Friday, and it was about seven in the evening. I made a right on to Delaware, and there was a lull in the traffic. I jumped on the gas pedal and slapped second gear which brought out a loud scream from the tires. I backed off the throttle. That was when Janice reminded me that there was a break in period for the engine. She asked, "Where are we going first?" We were on the road to show off our new vehicle. We made the rounds to parents and friends, but no one could be as excited as we were. We finally arrived at our upstairs apartment. We had to leave our new baby and go to bed. We did not know that this would be the kickoff to an amazing year.

The summer was long and hot and full of drives for ice cream and hot dogs and french fries. We had many hot afternoons to wash and wax the car and to enjoy with each other. Janice would be on a blanket catching sunrays while I was washing and waxing. Dad had caused a habit to evolve when he handed me that first can of wax with my first car. It has been that way ever since.

I was really enjoying the drives to the Naval Reserve meetings. I had to drive along the lake on a perfect road for a good-handling car. It was hilly and winding all around, and it was great fun.

The days were growing shorter, and the nights were getting cooler. Fall was bleeding into winter and our first snowfall. The snow began to fall as we left our apartment in Hamburg to have dinner with Dad and Mom. As we got closer to their house, the snow fell in greater quantity. They lived closer to the lake, so that was pretty normal. It was Saturday, and we were all relaxing in the evening. I was standing in the front door of the little house where I grew up. The bottom half of the door was closed and the top half was open. We all called it "the horse door." The storm door was closed. I was looking out through the glass of the storm door at the snow falling outside and the fireplace crackling behind me. It was beautiful, but I did not live here anymore. My memories were playing back like a DVD in my head: the sounds, the smell of burning wood, and suddenly, the vision I saw was in real life. As a boy, I had seen many dogs try to knock off Dad's garbage cans. This very night as I looked out the door through the snow, there was a black dog ready to do it again. It was as if an automatic pilot engaged in my head. I thought of all the ways that Dad and I had to scare the dogs away. The idea of throwing snowballs at dogs was mine. Dad would scare them off using fire-crackers once in a while. I decided to combine the two. I watched the dog under the streetlight at the end of the driveway. He stood out so well against the perfect, white snowfall. I quietly made my way out the door to Dad's garage. He always had some kind of firecrackers out there on a shelf. I grabbed a cherry bomb from the shelf with its stiff green fuse sticking straight out. My plan was to pack the cherry bomb inside of a snowball with the fuse sticking out. I would light the fuse with the cigarette lighter from my new car and throw it near the dog. Maybe the dog would think it was gunfire and never come back. This was way too much logic to expect from a dog. I was on a mission and focused.

I quietly approached the car while I stayed in the shadows. I brushed the snow from the car door and opened it. The interior light came on, but the dog was so focused he did not notice. I reached in and pushed the cigarette lighter down so it would heat up. I continued to pack the snow around the cherry bomb and left it only with the fuse exposed. The lighter popped up signify-ing that it had reached temperature. I reached into the car and pulled it out of the socket. I left the door open as I stepped about six to ten feet away from the car. I had the snowball in my right hand and the lighter in my left hand. It was time to touch the lighter to the green fuse sticking out of the snowball. It began to spark. I reared my right hand back for a good throw. At that very instant, the snowball broke apart, and the cherry bomb flew out of it and straight into our Mustang—it was like it had a mission of its own.

It bounced off of the driver's seat and bounced on the orange, rubber floor mat as the sparks flew from the fuse. It continued to roll down near the gas pedal and stopped right there. Terror entered my heart and mind at exactly the same time. I made a lunge for the car, and something stood me straight up. I went to grab the cherry bomb, but I could not get my hand to move. I grabbed the car door to shut it. I could not shut it because something was keeping the door from moving. That was when a thought ran and threw my head: "If you shut the door, the windows will be blown out." Three physical things happened, and then the, message got in my brain. What occupied my mind now was the certainty of the destruction of our first new car. I turned my back to the car, and the explosion happened. This must of all happened in about four heartbeats.

The noise attracted everyone to the front door of Dad's house. They saw me standing in a huge cloud of smoke with the car door open. I began to turn back towards the car—fully expecting to see the worst. Little pieces of hot paper were now falling on me. I thought they were pieces of the interior of the car. They were the wading from the cherry bomb. As the smoke began to clear, I was astounded to see the interior fully intact. I put my head into the car and could see a slight dent in the floor where the cherry bomb had laid. That was it! I stood up and coughed as I walked to the other side of the car to open the door to let the smoke out. That was when someone yelled from the house. "What happened?" I turned and said softly, "A miracle."

I walked back into Dad's house and sat down on the couch. I took a deep breath and explained what I had planned to do. I now had a chance to think of how I had been protected from even more injuries. Dad interrupted my silence with a question: "Did you learn anything?"

I was now at a very different point in life, where others actually depended on me. I could no longer do silly things without a thought. It could cost me a great deal financially, physically, and emotionally. Now, my actions had lasting effects on others and me.

The dog had just walked off when the cherry bomb went off. I had let the dog control my actions.

God's grace saved me from injury and the car from costly damage. He grabbed my attention again. We learned that Janice, the love of my life, was now pregnant with our first child.

Christmas came, and the season was as glorious as ever. We had decided to go to church with my Dad and Mom. Christmas Eve came, and we drove to Dad's house. I did not feel like going to church. I had already forgotten what happened five weeks before. Janice said that it did not matter how I felt because we needed to go. Now, I was even more irritated because she was on their side. What a dumb thought!

That evening the astronauts came on to the TV with a live broadcast from space. They were on their way to the moon. They were to orbit the moon for the first time. The next mission would be the moon landing. This was preparation for the next mission. As we watched, the astronauts took a camera shot of the moon from the spacecraft and then, the earth. Then they began to read from Genesis 1. They completed their reading by saying "Merry Christmas and God bless everyone on the good earth." I was moved in my heart. How foolish I was to let feelings interfere with what was right and good. They reminded me again of the true reason for Christmas. Where was my heart and brain? We knew at that moment that the world had changed. It was changed on the first Christmas, and it had changed again tonight, on this Christmas.

In the days ahead, the winter had changed to spring, and the spring changed to summer. America had put men on the moon.

Our own lives were changing so much because of that. We found that our food was changing and how we prepared it. Most of all, it taught us that dreams do come true when you believe enough to work at them believing they will come true.

Janice and I now had our own family, and that was first above all else. That is change. We were no longer alone with just the two of us.

Follow His Incense to His Essence

All of us make decisions every day. We just do not know that decisions change our very lives and us. We were about to change our lives.

Janice and I had talked about moving to Charlotte, North Carolina, for a number of years. We were going there four to five times a year. It was always very nice.

Janice and I began every week by attending church at Southtowns Christian Center. It continues to be a very uplifting place.

We entered the sanctuary and sat about five rows from the back. The worship service was already underway. The sanctuary seats were full.

When the entire service was ended, Janice and I stood up to leave. I felt a soft tap on my right shoulder. I turned in the direction of the tap. Janice turned at the same time because she saw the hand doing the tapping. We were both looking at a woman in her mid-thirties. We had never seen her before this moment. She looked at both of us and said, "I have never done this before. I am supposed to tell you to be bold. I do not know what it means but you do. Be bold! Have a blessed day." I said, "Thank you." Janice and I turned to put on our coats. We turned back towards the lady, but she was gone. I meant gone from the building and our sight.

Janice and I both knew what this meant to our lives at this time. We walked out of church discussing what she had said to us.

I was thinking of leaving a job I had done for twenty-four years and working our business full-time. We were also thinking of moving from Western New York to the Charlotte, North Carolina area.

We made the decision to leave the job that Sunday. I submitted the paperwork at the school the following Monday. That very action set into motion a whole series of events. Decisions always do that. I knew by now that decisions can change your course but not your destination.

We were into the sunshine of spring, and it was Sunday. We arrived at church early enough to get seats five rows from the front.

Janice and I were into the singing and worship very quickly. It always made you come alive covering you with a joyful feeling. I was singing with my eyes closed because I did not want to be distracted by my surroundings. My nostrils sent a message to my brain. It said that something was burning. The odor became stronger and stronger. It was the wonderful smell of incense. I thought how wonderful it was that they burn incense during worship. It became so strong that I knew it was burning right near me. I opened my eyes to see. I looked all around the sanctuary. I could not see that incense was burning anywhere. I looked for a wisp of smoke or some kind of flame. There was none to be seen. I sniffed the air deeply a number of times. The scent was still very strong. Janice looked at me and said, "Are you all right?" I said, "Yes, but someone is burning incense. Can you smell it?" She answered, "No, but that is the presence of the Lord, and it must be just for you!" I was stunned because I knew she was right.

The worship part of the service was ending, and the essence of incense was fading with it. I wanted it all back.

Pastor Tom was teaching his message and ended with a prayer. We all went into prayer. The essence of incense returned like a wave rolling over me. It was the same strength as before. I sensed fullness and completion and the warmth of great love. As our prayers ended, the essence diminished and then left. I was exhausted but filled with joy. Janice and I walked out of church talking about my experience. I wanted it to be like this every day. She reminded me that these bodies could not survive that experience that often.

Our lives continued. We experienced a magnificent summer, which was now turning into fall. I was really pondering on my life, and I knew I had to do more with it. I was forty-nine and still trying to find my purpose.

The fall leaves were falling and so was my attitude. I was progressing down the path of depression which I had never experienced before. I was going lower and lower—emotionally. I thought of the times I observed people who were depressed, and I wanted to tell them to get over it. I now knew what those people were feeling. I knew the physical pain one feels in the belly. I had a new understanding of stress and anxiety.

I knew I had to find a job because our business was going downhill. I started asking myself why I was such a fool. What have I done to my wife and my family? I no longer trusted my decisions or myself.

This all served to drive me to my knees. It was the only thing left. I had no solution. I was praying like never before. Janice kept reminding me that this to shall pass. She still believed in me when I could not.

The year seemed to drag on so slowly. The business did not grow. I continued to pray, and so did Janice. It was now summer but unlike any other summer.

We would awake in the morning and get dressed. We would stand and face each other. Then we would hug and hold each other as we prayed out loud. This became a habit, and we have continued it to this day.

It was now August, and it was a bright, sunny morning. We went through our morning routine, and I showered for my job at a local hardware store. While I was in the shower, the phone rang. I did not hear it ring, so Janice answered. The only thing I could hear was Janice yelling and opening the bathroom door. She was extremely excited.

She explained that the principal of a high school twenty miles south of Charlotte had called. He said, "I have conducted a national search for an industrial technology teacher. I have decided that Ted is my man. Could you please have him call me back at two p.m. for a phone interview?" I jumped out of the shower wrapped the towel around me. We held each other and laughed and wept at the same time.

I returned the call, and after a few questions on references, he said, "As far as I am concerned, you are hired. When can you be here?" I told him I needed three weeks to make arrangements. He was very accommodating, and I really appreciated it.

Three weeks later, I was moved to the Charlotte area. Janice stayed at our home up north. Janice's parents were kind enough to give me a bedroom at their home.

I started down that downward spiral again. I missed my very best friend in life so much it hurt. We talked on the phone, which really helped, but I missed my son and my daughter and our grandchildren with a passion also.

It was about two months later that my daughter Tawnya moved down. I was so happy to meet her at the train station in Charlotte. This also meant that I had to move over to Randy and Denise's house. They had a basement apartment in their home which provided much more room. They were wonderful, and I think they could tell I was not my usual upbeat self. Tawnya's arrival was a greatly needed uplift. After much talking, we both slept real well that night. We were both exhausted from the tension in our lives, self-inflicted or otherwise. It was truly great to see her.

We were now approaching Thanksgiving time, and Janice would be moving down that week. Piece by piece, our family was coming back together. Wade and Lori would not be moving down with their two children. I talked to Wade once a week and missed him Lori, Stephen, and Kyra very much.

Janice tried to sell our house since August. She said that ten couples came and looked but no offers were made. She decided to come south with me. Brian—the son of my lifelong friend Tom—said that he would stay at the house while we were gone. That was a blessing for him and us.

Mike and Colleen are our very close friends. Colleen drove down with Janice and brought some more of our stuff down. We have been blessed with friends who were very loyal. It became very obvious at this strained time in our lives.

Thanksgiving was coming and so was Christmas, and we knew that we had to head north with Tawnya to see Wade, Lori, and the kids. It was so wonderful to be with them. I treasured every hour with them. I pledged to myself to appreciate them more in the coming years.

We were now going back home once a month to be with our family and go to our church. We both missed our pastor and church family.

Janice and I knew where we really belonged, and we needed to be back there. We talked about it on every trip we made. We had experienced enough of what we thought we wanted. The drives back south were becoming harder and harder. We both knew what we really wanted. Knowing what you want is much different than thinking what you want.

It was now the end of March, and it was a Saturday morning. The only people in the house were Randy and I. Randy was working in his office which was right next to our living quarters.

I was kneeling in prayer at the edge of the sofa. The sun was starting its climb for the day. The sky was a cloudless powder blue. The back of the sofa was against three double-hung windows. The windows looked out over a valley which dropped down twenty feet below the windows. The trees were just beginning to bud, so you could see the creek which flowed down the center of the valley. The sun seemed to shine right down the valley on a normal day. This would not be a normal day!

I ended my prayers and stood up at the front of the sofa. I was facing the windows and looking out at the valley full of trees and sunlight. I was admiring God's beautiful work when I noticed something different. A wisp of smoke was drifting slowly down the valley from right to left. Then I realized this was not a smoke trail but rather a small cloud. This caused me to look farther up the valley. There was a cloud formation moving slowly in a rolling manner down the valley. I stepped to the door. I noticed there was no breeze. The birds were silent and not a sound could be heard. The cloud was very white and becoming denser as it slowly moved down the valley toward me. I sniffed the air for a smell, but there was none. I took a step forward, and a feeling of great awe came upon me. I stopped in my tracks and stood as my mind became fearful, but my heart was full of great joy and anticipation. My heart was racing while my mind was saying this was an experience. It was as if my mind and my heart were having this conversation but not a sound could be heard. I wanted to step forward, but I could not. The leading edge of the cloud was now straight in front of me. The cloud had become very thick and was now starting to block out the sunlight from the valley floor. There was no breeze, and it was total silence. Was I dreaming, or was it all real? It was all very real. That was when I thought that someone else had to see this. I wanted a witness of this sight.

I turned and ran into the house and to Randy's office, which took only about a few seconds. I demanded that he look out the window of his office, which had the same view as my windows. He looked out the window, and before he could say anything, I knew his answer. I knew this vision was only for me. At that moment, he said, "What am I looking for?" The cloud that had filled the valley was totally gone. I stared at the sunlight beaming down the valley. Randy just shook his head as I turned and walked back into our living area. I walked over to the windows and looked out at the bright sunlight that had been blocked by the cloud, and I asked myself, "Why didn't you walk out into the cloud?" Then I answered, "I was fearful of a great power that I knew was in it!"

I knew that it was His presence in the cloud, and it gave me great joy as I dropped to my knees and wept by the edge of the sofa. At that moment, I felt so humble and small and yet so grateful for the experience.

I came to the conclusion that the Lord was letting me know that He was with me. The sight of Him was more than enough. This had to be how the Hebrews felt in the desert when the cloud protected them by day and the pillar of fire at night.

Two weeks later, I was awakened at about three in the morning. It was a thought that was so strong that it was almost audible. It kept repeating: "You have to tell them. You have to tell them today." It kept repeating for at least half an hour. I finally answered out loud, "Okay, I will!" Then it stopped.

I knew that it meant that I had to tell the school district I was not going to be returning in the fall.

I went to school that morning. I was preparing the shop for the students when something told me to check the hallway. I went over to the door and opened it. I looked to the left. The principal was about five steps away from the door. He looked at me and said, "I was just coming to see you. Are you coming back to us in the fall?" I said, "I need to talk with you." He answered, 'I thought that might be the case. I just had a feeling." He was a man of faith also, and I knew he knew.

I went to his office that afternoon and told him I would not be back. He looked me in the eye and said, "You are one of the best I have ever seen, and I will write that in a letter of recommendation." I was very grateful to have worked with Dr. Gummerson. He was a man of integrity. I was blessed greatly by him.

There was a release of great weight off of both Janice and I as the decision to move back north was put into motion. A decision made in prayer will do that.

Janice was waiting at the living quarters to hear how it all went. I returned at about four in the afternoon and told her about the day and the meeting with the principal. We both held each other and wept tears of gratitude and joy. We were going home!

The next day, I made a phone call to the city of Buffalo schools. I wanted find out who was the head of industrial arts/technology. I was told who to ask for.

Mr. Clap was the head of the technology department for the city of Buffalo. I called and explained my situation. He was very kind and asked for a description of my background. I heard him take a deep breath. Then he said, "As far as I am concerned, you are hired. Send me your credentials and call me when you are back in town."

I hung up the phone and smiled at Janice and said, "We are going home."

We could not pack up fast enough. We were going home to our children and grandchildren. We would never take our time with them for granted again. The ability to just take fifteen minutes and go see them was a cherished treat. We were all looking forward to any of the holidays together.

Mr. Clap was an excellent department head, and I will always be thankful for his kindness and blessing. There was no question of how this all came together and who actually orchestrated the events. It certainly was not me.

Wade and Lori now have five children, and we see them often, at least once a week. In the summer, we have water balloon wars, we go fishing, swimming, play various outdoor games, and have barbecues continuously. Wade, Lori, Stephen, Kyra, Lucas, Nathan, and Nick, along with Tawnya, Tom, Tommy, and Gracie Kate are helping to keep us young. There is a lot of laughter and joyous yelling and hooting coming from our woods and yard. That is what the neighbors tell us.

We all look forward to the changing seasons and love the changes they bring to our daily routines. When winter comes, the games change from water balloons to snowballs and sledding. The barbecues become buffets in the dining rooms of Wade's, Tawnya's, or our house.

Janice and I are truly blessed. Our grandchildren actually love being around us, and we love teaching them. That is our mission and our calling. We continue to follow His incense to this day!

REVEALING OF THE ROOTS

I think that we all ask ourselves the big question at some point in our lives: Where do we come from in our family history? What are our roots? Some people do not want to know. I was not one of those people.

One evening, we received a phone call from a business mentor in South Carolina. Dom asked an amazing question. He asked, "Would you and Janice like to go to Poland and do a business seminar for my marketing organization in Poland?" It took less than a minute to say yes. Dom and Pat trusted us enough to talk to their business group in Poland. We were both honored and humbled at the same time. Dom continued to explain the details of the trip. We were to land in Krakow and do the function there. We just were excited to be going on such a journey.

The departure day finally came. We boarded a plane from Buffalo to Chicago. Once we were in Chicago, we boarded our flight on LOT Polish Airlines for Krakow, Poland. The adventure was underway. There were many people on the flight who were going home and just a few tourists. Polish and English were spoken on the aircraft by the crew and on all instructions. As I listened to all the conversations, I was reminded of all the conversations at my grandma's house. The Polish phrases were all coming back to me. It was extremely exciting because I thought I had forgotten the words. Janice and I both noticed how polite everyone was far more than usual.

The plane lifted off and immediately, people pulled down their window shades. This was our first time on a flight to Europe. So this was new and different.

The pilot announced that we had reached our assigned altitude. It seemed as if everyone pulled his or her window shades down at once. I looked around and saw that everyone was preparing for sleep. There were a lot of experienced travelers. I looked at Janice and said, "I think we should do the same." Janice said, "I think we are both too excited to sleep, but we need to."

We were flying east, so we would be landing in the morning of the next day. We took off from Chicago at about eight in the evening, so we should be landing at about seven in the morning. Our flight path was being shown on a monitor along with the speed and altitude at the front of our cabin. We watched as we gathered our pillows and blankets from the storage areas. The challenge was to calm down enough to actually sleep. The plane quickly became really quiet as everyone else chased after the sleep they needed.

The activity of other passengers, hours later, told us that we were nearing our destination. Everyone was preparing for breakfast to be served. There was an air of excitement in the air that could actually be felt. You could sense the joy of returning home to the people and land that you love. The plane was filled with the glowing faces of joyful people. The plane must have seemed lighter to fly with all this joy lifting it. What a wonderful thing to witness. We were done with breakfast, and the cabin was buzzing with the preparation for landing. The pilot said we were on final approach. The cabin became very quiet and still. Janice and I were looking out the window at the cloud cover. We decided to just sit back and relax. We could feel the aircraft's wheels touch earth gently. It was a smooth landing. The cabin was still quiet as the plane came to a stop about half a mile from the terminal. We could see two buses pull up about fifty yards from the plane as we were unbuckling our seatbelts. It seemed as if everyone stood up together and started clapping. The man behind us explained that this was the custom. The passengers were honoring the captain and the crew for the safe trip they had provided us. I could not help but think on how appreciative that really was. Janice and I had never experienced that before. I looked at the man who explained this to us and said, "Wow." He looked back at me and said, "Welcome to Poland."

People were laughing and joking as we made our way to the exit and the gangway. As we turned to exit the plane, I looked down the stairs of the gangway and noticed two soldiers at the bottom with their weapons. We walked by them on the way to board the waiting buses. Once we were on the buses, it was a short ride to the terminal. One of the other passengers explained that the planes were not let close to the terminal for security reasons. The buses came to a stop, and we had about ten steps to a door that was held open by a soldier.

The bright daylight was changed to a large darkened room about the size of a small gym. I noticed total silence as we entered this place. These once happy people went silent and formed perfectly straight lines at what looked like tollbooths on the expressway. The only light in the room came from these two booths. Inside them were soldiers. They looked very angry to every person who approached the window of the booth. I was told to look the soldier straight in the eyes and not to smile and only answer the question firmly. There was to be no conversation with anyone—anywhere in this room. As I approached the window, I slid my passport through the hole in the window and stood silent. The soldier looked at my passport then glared at me. They looked back down and then at my face and clothing. He slid the passport back to me and waved me through with his other hand. He did the same with Janice. We both took about five steps to a door and stepped back out into the happy people we had seen before we entered that room. We entered 1946 when we entered that room and came back into the present when we exited that room. It was an experience every American should have. I was so glad to be born in America. We both knew we were protected through our faith in this whole experience.

We were looking for the signs that said Baggage as we continued to walk through the airport. We saw the smiling faces of Vitek and Ella walking toward us. They gave Janice and me a big hug and asked us how the flight was. We had met Vitek and Ella when they were in Charlotte on business. They were really good people. They had and still have a very sweet spirit.

Vitek said he had some people he wanted us to meet. He turned and about ten smiling faces walked up. He introduced us to them all. They were certainly excited people. They all helped and carried our luggage. Everyone was warm to us on this chilly but sunny morning. Vitek asked if we would like to go for some kava (that is coffee in Poland). We said that that would be great. We got into Vitek's Land Cruiser and took a ten-minute ride to what looked like a normal, two-story house. I did not notice a sign or anything. We got out of the Land Cruiser and started walking toward the front door. Vitek turned and said softly, "This is one of our coffeehouses. It is different from America." As we entered the front door, we turned left and walked into what looked like the dining room of a home. It was set up with four small tables. We moved them together forming one table. Janice and I sat in the middle seats so that we could hear and talk to everyone.

These people were very excited about life. You could just feel it. We were about to witness a hunger for knowledge and truth like I had never seen before.

The owner of the coffee shop served us all coffee or tea. Then the first questions from the group were things like "What state are you from?" and "How many children do you have?" and "Where do they live?" This opened the door to the real questions. The group was now starting to lean in toward Janice and me—physically. Then it happened like an explosion: the questioning became very rapid. The group was on the edge of their seats, literally. The breathing even got faster. They asked, "Where do Americans get their dreams from? What do you do to stay excited about life? How do you get and keep strong faith? Do you believe in God?" Their concentration level was extreme. The group looked deep into our eyes the entire time. No one was looking out the windows at the sunshine. They felt the answers could help change their lives. Someone said, "We want to know because you are from the land of opportunity—the promised land." The questions came at us as fast as you just read them. It was a rapid-fire questioning out of pure excitement. Janice and I had never seen such a hunger for information on living a good productive life. The people wanted to know the books we read and how many. They were looking for our commitment to improving ourselves. This was a very emotional experience for the two of us. We had sat for an hour when Vitek asked if we would like to see some of Krakow. We told him yes.

Janice and I looked at each other with a look of pure exhaustion because we got only about two good hours of sleep in the last forty-eight hours. We were now running on adrenaline. We both knew this whole situation was the chance of a lifetime, and we were not going to waste it on sleep. We would just sleep when we get home.

We were back in the Land Cruiser riding down some streets of Krakow when Vitek asked, "Would you like to see a real eight-hundred-year-old castle? We are taking you to the fortress where the Polish kings lived. The communists took it over, but now, it is open to public tours." Vitek then explained that, at one time, Poland had the best universities in all of Europe. The abundance of Polish jokes in America popped into my head. These people are very intelligent and hard working. The truth was the exact opposite of the jokes.

We were walking by a statue of Copernicus, which the people were very proud of.

We continued our walk up a long inclined road. It led to the main gate of the castle. The road was made up of very large stones which were worn out by the hundreds of years of use. We turned to the left after entering the gate and continued on our history-revealing walk. Our next stop was the church which the kings attended. You had to walk up three stone steps to two very large wooden carved doors. The doors were opened for us, and we quietly and respectfully entered. The quietness was almost deafening once inside. The acoustics were so good that you could hear everyone whispering. There were no seats, and the floors were worn where people had stood for hundreds of years. The black stones were literally cupped two inches deep where people stood. There were rows of cupped stones. The walls had gorgeous carvings of scenes from the Bible. Many were incidents in the life of Jesus. They were carvings in the stone. It was truly beautiful.

Vitek said we had to get going, so we made our way back to the car while receiving more history along the way. Ella asked if we were ready to eat, and we certainly were. We were back in the land rover riding to the restaurant which was an hour northwest of Krakow. It looked like a low log cabin as we parked in front of it. Once we entered, Vitek explained that this restaurant was over six hundred years old. The log ceilings were very low because the people were much shorter when it was first built. I also noticed carvings in the logs. One of them was the numbers 1606 and a person's name. What a feeling to be in a place that was centuries old. Janice handed me a menu, which was in Polish and English. I was surprised it was in both. The waitress asked if I was American, and when I said yes, she smiled and said she loved America and hoped to go there one day. I ordered potato pancakes because I was concerned about the food and how my body would react. The conversation was back to the questions on America and free enterprise and the influence of faith on our business as we waited for our food to come. My pancakes arrived, and after a forkful, I smiled. Ella said, "They must be good." Then

I said, "They are just like my grandmothers." Grandma had pre-pared me for this trip years before, and neither of us knew it. And then again, maybe she did!

Janice and I finished our meal and headed back to the Land Cruiser. Vitek asked, "Would you like to see a salt mine?" We said that we would. He pointed across the street to a building which looked like a tourist-welcoming center. It was the entrance to the eight-hundred-foot-deep salt mine. It was also about eight hundred years old. Vitek purchased the tickets, and we proceeded to a doorway which led to a stairway that was hewn out of oak. It spiraled down about ten levels where we were told to wait for the group to assemble. Our guide then informed us of the age of the mine and gave us more history. The guide took us down a cor-ridor which was carved out of the salt. The salt was gray in color. It looked like a piece of pavement from a road, but it had some shining particles on it. The guide explained that it was refining that made the salt white. The tunnels were quite large in diame-ter. The guide told us that this was so that horses could be used to haul loads of salt through them. It was explained that, eventually, horses were born and raised in the depths of the mine because it was too hard and too time-consuming to get them in and out of the mine. The horses were much calmer, and they got used to the mine's noise when they grew up. It was hard to imagine that these horses never saw the light of day.

We came to another staircase which was taking us to a lower level. We were already one hundred feet under the ground, and now, we were going deeper. We came to another area where the guide explained more about how the mine procedures went. There were some miners whose job was to carry a bird in a cage down to test for poisoned air. Some carried a flame on a long rod to test areas for methane gas. This was not a good place to work hun-dreds of years ago. However, the salt was in huge demand, and it was very valuable. That was where the saying "Worth a man's weight in salt" came from. People were even paid in salt sometimes. That was the origin for the word *salary*. You talk about history coming alive.

It was time to descend down some more stairs. When we stepped off the staircase, we were now about four hundred feet down. We could feel the difference in the air, but it was hard to explain. The guide said that people with asthma would live down here for months and breathe much better. There was an area that was like a hospital for the people with asthma to stay in.

We walked down this one tunnel which led to a huge chapel that was carved completely out of salt. The chandeliers and wall frescos were all salt. There were no pews, and the floors were so shiny you thought they were marble. It was all salt. It was all magnificent to see such work and dedication. We were shown an underground pond. It was crystal clear water.

We ended our tour at a gift shop where we purchased some amber eggs. This was where you had to make a choice of walking the six hundred feet to the surface on stairs or taking an elevator. We took the elevator, and that was a story to itself.

The elevator cars held only four people per car. There were four cars stacked one upon the other. It was like a train—only vertical. We were in the first car. The elevator would move and stop to load the next car. Once the fourth car was filled, we proceeded up. There was no light anywhere. This bothered some people, but I just closed my eyes, and it all seemed natural. The cars made many clunking and clicking sounds, and you could hear the people in the cars below us. The blackness was almost felt physically. It was like thick, black velvet encapsulating us. You could see the light as we approached the surface. When the doors opened, you almost bolted from the car. Everyone else had the same reaction. Some people stood and breathed deeply after exiting the elevator car because they were in such stress. Now, I understood why the ticket taker asked if Janice and I were claustrophobic at the beginning of the tour.

We were back in the visitor's center, and the light of day looked wonderful. The light was dwindling as the sun was about to go below the horizon. Vitek said, "We need to hit the road. The function has been moved from Krakow to about twenty miles south of Poznan." I never thought of what he had just said. The significance would hit us later.

We were still in the outskirts of Krakow, and I noticed that people would stare as we drove by. I asked Vitek why, and he said, "The Land Cruiser is a very big vehicle in Poland, and only very important people would be in such a vehicle." As he was speaking, I noticed the abundance of Ladas and a few other small cars. Lada was a version of Fiat. What stuck out was how they were all gray, black, silver, or white. The red green or blue ones were not to be seen. This was a reminder of the blandness of life under the communists. It still was on the minds of the people. The streets were very clean and so were the people. They were at the bus stops waiting. There was order and patience in their eyes as they were returning home from work in the city.

We were about to get on the expressway when Vitek pointed and said, "That is a Ford dealership." I looked and saw a small, two-story house of about six hundred square feet. There were no cars around it, and no cars near it. Vitek said, "If you want a car, you must order it and wait a year to receive it. You order from a catalog." The people here must have patience to survive. We entered the expressway which was very much an extension of the German autobahn. If you were driving below eighty miles an hour, you stayed in the right lane. Some very fast cars would pass us at one hundred or more.

Vitek got off the expressway to stop at a McDonald's restaurant. It was very contemporary in design and very expensive by Polish standards. There were no children inside. This restaurant was considered a luxury here.

We were back on the road. Before the sun had gone down, I got a good look at the countryside. It seemed to be missing any heavily wooded areas. It was consumed over thousands of years for heat and housing. There were lots of rolling hillsides of grass. The darkness was upon us as we were now off of the expressway and on to the country roads. We were really flying along on very narrow roads. Vitek was very familiar with them. He was driving fast but safely. The houses were not made of wood. They were made of a cement stucco kind of construction. There was no color but gray. We could see them in the headlights. They were the same back in Krakow.

We were run through small villages every five or ten miles. The roads would become narrower, and the front doors were literally opening on to the streets. In fact, I thought if a person opens the front door of their house when we are passing, the Land Cruiser would take it off. Janice said, "I think we are in a James Bond movie." That was exactly how it felt.

We finally arrived at a small university outside of Poznan. Vitek pulled up to the front of what Ella called a college-dormitory-type building. Janice and I got out of the Land Cruiser and walked through the front door. The experience was a shock to the eyes, spirit, and mind. We were transported back to 1946.

A black wire came out of a hole in the ceiling. It hung down about four feet from the ceiling. On the end of it was a bare lightbulb of about forty watts. There was no shade or decorations on it. It was the only light in the entrée room. It lifted the darkness but only slightly. To our left was an enclosed area for an office surrounded by frosted glass. Vitek was talking to someone in that room. It was quiet and shadowy. All of the woodwork was dark brown, and the walls were painted a lighter shade of brown. The effect was very dismal. Vitek came out of the room and started walking ahead of us. He motioned for us to follow him down this darkened hallway. There was a door at the end of the hallway which was almost completely absent of the light. Vitek opened the door, and the hallway was bathed in very bright light. It was like a shaft of light coming out of heaven. We stepped through the door and into the present. The walls had white marble paneling with a swirl of what looked like gold. The hallway glowed. It was a stunning change. Our faces showed our surprise to Vitek and Ella. Vitek said, "When the communists were in charge, this is where the leaders stayed. The rest of the people did not matter." This section of the dorm was where we were staying. The contrast had to be experienced to be fully appreciated.

Our room had two beds, a TV with one channel, and a bathroom with a shower. Each bed had a down-filled comforter which was about five inches thick. These comforters were very warm, just like Grandma's was. We crawled under those comforters at about four in the morning. We were both exhausted but still very excited about all that was happening.

The morning greeted us with a little bit of sun, but it soon became cloudy. It was about nine in the morning when there was a knock at the door. Ella was standing there when Janice opened the door. She said, "Are you ready for breakfast?" We certainly were. We gathered up all our notes for the business seminar we would be doing later that afternoon and followed Ella out the door.

Vitek was waiting at the Land Cruiser with the doors open. We hopped in and were off on our adventure. Vitek drove through the city to the house of one of his business group leaders. We arrived under a graying sky and were entering a house of the same color. The front door opened and revealed a smiling face and all the wonderful smells of a big breakfast. We walked across a light yellow, hardwood floor made up of eight-inch-wide planks. The floor glistened with its clear finish. The owner said that the wood was a hundred years old. It had no creaks and seemed to be as solid as cement. As we approached a dining table, we walked on beautiful, handmade rugs. The light- colored floors accented with the royal blues, burgundy, emerald green, and deep red rugs gave a joyful feeling to the house. The contrast with the exterior of the house could not have been greater.

The furniture was of the vintage 1950s and 1960s style, but it looked brand new in the spring of year 2001.

We were led to a large, handcrafted, wooden dining room table. It was covered with a deep, dark blue tablecloth which had white, knitted cloth webbing all around the edges.

We sat down at the table which was surrounded by smiling faces. We were served Polish sausages, scrambled eggs, sour dough toast, potato pancakes with applesauce, and cheese-filled perogys. I carefully tasted each item. I thought that grandma had to be cooking in the kitchen. It hit me at that very moment. Grandma Malinowski grew up in this region of Poland. She used all of these recipes in her preparations of food. This was a revelation but only the first of many. Something was unfolding right before our eyes, and no person could arrange that which was unfolding.

The owners of the house were very happy with the joy they gave us at breakfast. I told them they were a blessing to us.

It was time to proceed to the site of the business seminar that was about a half hour away. The location was an auditorium on a college campus.

We got out of the Land Cruiser and were escorted through the building doors by Vitek and Ella. Vitek introduced us to the translators. Janice and I each had one each when we were speaking. We were then taken to the seats in the front row of the audience. Our translators sat next to us when the event began. Vitek introduced Janice and I to the group of seven hundred people. There was a lot of cheering and hand clapping. I thanked everyone for their kind greeting and introduced Janice to speak first. She did some great teaching and then turned the stage over to me. She went to her seat in the front row next to her translator and sat down. I had worked on my notes before we came, but for some reason, I was compelled to blurt out a question. "Who here believes in God?" I said. It just leaped off of my lips. The response was an immediate explosion of rising hands. There was no hesitation. I was stunned at the response. I then stated that I was glad we now had a man with morals and character in the White House. The entire room exploded from their seats with a standing ovation. I stood in awe. I thought of how this never happened in America. It was a truly stunning experience in the spring of 2001. I finally collected myself and got into some teaching on leadership. Janice was having a conversation with her translator while I was speaking. The translator asked her if we had any relatives in Poland. Janice explained to him that I had cousins in Poland. The translator asked where my cousins lived. Janice pulled the envelope from her purse with my cousins' address on it and gave it to him. The address was in Poznan. The building we were in was about twenty minutes from the address on the letter. The translator looked at the address and looked back at Janice twice. He had a totally stunned look on his face as he said, "I know these people. They live about five houses from my grandparents. I have been to their house. I will call them and invite them to the leadership meeting tomorrow."

I finished my talk, and Janice told me what had happened. Her voice quivered as she spoke. We held each other and wept. We both knew that only one person could have put this whole chain of events together. We both thanked Him at that very moment.

We left the function and arrived at a former government house which had been converted to a restaurant. It was like walking into a small palace in the 1800s. It was extremely ornate with heavy burgundy curtains trimmed in gold thread. The furniture was Victorian in style with red velvet seat cushions. We were told that much of the decorating was left from the government. We were the only people in the restaurant. When we finished dinner, we walked through the village square. Ella stopped at the window of the shoe store. She was excited because there were five pairs of shoes in the window. She said, "That is the entire inventory of the store. Last month, they had three pairs." The shoes were all black and all the same style. We looked in other store windows and found similar limited displays. All of the shops were closed at five in the afternoon on a Saturday. Vitek said, "That is better than being closed three days a week. Things are slowly improving."

We walked to the Land Cruiser to return for the evening function. Janice's translator met us at our seats and said, "I called your relatives, and two of them will be here tomorrow to meet you." Our eyes filled with warm tears as we held each other and said, "Thank you Lord." Janice looked me in the eyes and asked, "How does it feel to know that you will meet your heritage tomorrow?"

We did the evening function, which was the telling of our story. After the function, we were invited to the home of one of the leaders. The house was the typical gray on the outside and colorful and meticulously cleaned on the inside. We were led to a room. Two comfortable chairs were set at one end of the room. We sat down in those chairs and answered questions on business and life. There were about fifty people packed into that room. Suddenly, after about thirty minutes, the topic became faith. Everyone wanted to know an example of goal setting in the Bible. We talked about David and Goliath, and then, someone read the story. We stopped and broke down the story, and the people were stunned at the importance of the goal to David. Then they asked about dreams and aspirations.

These people were so hungry for life in the Word. The room seemed to be exploding with excitement. The excitement was caused by the realization that God was on their side, and He wanted abundance to overcome them. They confessed that they wanted to be better people and contribute to their country and their new freedom. They became emotional many times. Vitek announced that we had to end the session at about 3 a.m. He explained that we had a breakfast meeting in the morning at 9:00 a.m. Janice and I were both exhausted, but the fire in our hearts for these people burned strongly. What a magnificent feeling it was to know that you have been useful.

We arrived at our room, and the down-filled comforters on our beds caressed our bodies and warmed and loved on us. They served to recharge our batteries for the three hours of sleep we achieved.

Vitek and Ella knew we would need a phone call to get up. They did their duty and picked us up at 8:30 a.m.

We were invited to breakfast at another leader's house. When we arrived, there were about twenty people around the table, but I noticed that Vitek, Ella, Janice, and I were the only ones eating. The rest of the group continued the questions from the night before. They were not too proud to ask anything.

We left the house at about eleven, and we headed to the college campus for the leadership session. We entered a classroom that had chairs set up in theater style. There were about forty chairs.

Janice's translator approached us and told us that my cousins had arrived. He escorted us to them on the right side of the room. We needed the translator in order to talk. The cousins had brought pictures with them. They were brother and sister. They were about the same age as Janice and I. He owned a pharmaceutical warehouse, and she worked at the university. They explained to us that most of the family was involved in teaching or in the medical area as doctors. I was a teacher, as was my sister and my daughter. My mind just said, "So that's where that comes from." The family tended toward professionals. That was what my son is. It all seemed to answer many questions. The cousins brought out their pictures, and there she was. I thought it was my grandmother in one of the pictures. It was their grandmother. She was the twin sister of my grandmother. It was all so revealing and so astounding to be meeting them. We knew we were witnessing a miracle in our lives. We continued to talk through our translator for about twenty minutes. We had to stop and do our teaching. The cousins stayed through the whole thing. We talked of our families after the session hugged each other and parted.

The sheer exhaustion was now making itself known. We had to leave for Krakow right after the leadership talk. Darkness was beginning to fall like a curtain on a stage as we started down the road for Krakow.

There was much conversation on the road: open conversation. We felt that we could trust Vitek and Ella, and they felt the same way about us. Our lives had been in their hands for four days. "Why were the German death camps all located in Poland?" I asked Vitek. He answered, "Poland was the only country that openly accepted the Jews who left Palestine. Hitler wanted to punish Poland after he invaded."

It was now about 2 a.m. Vitek turned to me and said, "The police are around the bend in the road. I saw the car in the moonlight." As I turned to look out the windshield, I saw the white police car parked across the road. We had been going very fast. Ella began to describe each event about ten seconds before it happened. It was the greatest example of the value of experience. I must admit I was concerned until she started her descriptions. Ella said, "Vitek will stop the Land Cruiser and get out." He did. "Vitek is going to walk over to the police car and talk to the officer in the passenger seat." He did. "Now, he will walk around to the driver and talk to him." He did. "Vitek will now reach in his pocket and take out an American five dollar bill and give it to the driver." He did, and you could see the driver throw back his head and laugh as he waved for Vitek to leave. We could see it all play out as our headlights shined on the whole event. Vitek smiled as he walked back and got into the Land Cruiser. He put the machine in gear, and we were on our way again. I could not help myself. I asked Vitek, "They let you go for five dollars?" Vitek said, "Five American dollars will buy them five bottles of vodka. Under the old regime, the communists knew that the people were easier to rule if you kept them drunk. They just made sure that they kept the price of vodka very cheap." We were receiving lesson upon lesson from someone with real life experience.

We finally reached the house we would be sleeping at. Vitek said that it was near the airport. We would not have a long trip to the airport in the next afternoon. Vitek introduced us to the owners who were leaders in Vitek and Ella's business. We remembered seeing them at the function. They showed our tired bodies to the bedroom, and we saw those wonderful and inviting down-filled covers calling us to slumber. We answered with gratefulness.

We were awakened by bright sunlight and the smell of breakfast cooking. The comforters were about to give us a good-bye as we dressed for our flight back to America. We went down the white oak stairway and entered the main hallway of the house. This was a very large house by Polish standards. The owners were very proud and thankful. They gave us a tour after breakfast. The floors were all ten-inch-wide planks of white maple covered with colorful throw rugs. The contrast of the light-colored wood with the reds, greens, purple, and yellows in the rugs was simply stunning. All this was done by the owners. The outside was the standard gray stucco—hiding the beauty within. The owners said that they had paid cash each step of the way. We were looking at ten years of work, so far. They explained that this was the first year you could get a mortgage in Poland. They were very hard working people. It was now time to leave.

Vitek and Ella drove us to the airport, and about ten other people from their organization met us there. We all went to the restaurant area of the airport for some coffee. The parting became an emotional experience. In a matter of days, we had come to know a people who work hard, have deep faith, very patriotic to their country, and love what America is—the land where dreams come true.

Janice and I wept when we parted, and we wept again after we boarded the plane and were in our seats. We slept the entire flight of nine hours. When we landed in New York City, the passengers gave a standing ovation to the flight crew. Flying would never be the same again.

We have met great leaders in Dom, Pat, Dex, and Birdie many years before. This relationship resulted in the astounding experience we had just lived. My roots were clearly revealed by the great planner of all life. I did not know the plan—but He sure does. I know that it all started with a prayer many years before. It continues on to this day. It must be passed down to our children and their children. We must tell the stories of our lives. It is part of our purpose.

This is all part of becoming an American. I have a heritage, but I am now American, and my heritage led me to become an American. It has been stated that America is not a place but rather an idea. I believe that to be true. I now own the idea, and I want others to feel the joy of this idea. I must pass it on because it has been paid for by the lives of those that have gone before me.

I know that I am greatly blessed over and over. I know that we must all think on these things!